TAKING
YOUR TEAM
TO THE
TOP

HOW TO
BUILD AND MANAGE
GREAT TEAMS LIKE THE PROS

TED SUNDQUIST
WITH JUSTIN SPIZMAN

New York   Chicago   San Francisco   Lisbon   London   Madrid   Mexico City
Milan   New Delhi   San Juan   Seoul   Singapore   Sydney   Toronto

1 2 3 4 5 6 7 8 9 0   DOC/DOC   1 9 8 7 6 5 4 3

ISBN   978-0-07-180544-5
MHID   0-07-180544-3

e-ISBN   978-0-07-180545-2
e-MHID   0-07-180545-1

Library of Congress Cataloging-in-Publication Data

Sundquist, Ted.
  Taking your team to the top : how to build and manage great teams like the pros / by Ted Sundquist and Justin Spizman. – 1 Edition.
    pages cm
  ISBN-13: 978-0-07-180544-5 (alk. paper)
  ISBN-10: 0-07-180544-3 (alk. paper)
  1. Teams in the workplace–Management. I. Title.
  HD66.S86 2013
  658.4'022–dc23

                                                                    2013002474

McGraw-Hill Education books are available at special quantity discounts to use as premiums and sales promotions or for use in corporate training programs. To contact a representative, please visit the Contact Us pages at www.mhprofessional.com.

This book is printed on acid-free paper.

CONTENTS

INTRODUCTION

Dear Reader,

You hold in your hands an answer to what seems like a very simple question. However, scholars, educators, coaches, general managers, employers, leaders, and team builders have all worked and studied for endless years in the hope of finding this answer. It is not easy to come by, and there may be numerous paths by which one can obtain it. But here it is, in your hands, ready to be digested and implemented within your own experiences and situation. I have gravitated toward leadership positions all my life, and it took me more than 20 years in managerial and leadership roles to formulate this answer. The question I hope to answer in this book is: how can you build the greatest team possible and set that team up to succeed in the world of business? As I said, it's an easy enough question. However, the answer is something that few people have actually developed. It takes grit, success, failure, determination, perseverance, experience, and the help of many others.

I was educated and trained at the U.S. Air Force Academy, where the sole mission is to produce leaders for the Air Force. Leadership is inherently joined at the hip to teamwork and team building. I was fortunate enough to "cut my teeth" during three years as a flight commander in Germany and then as an assistant coach, and later head coach, in college football. Having been a college football player myself at the Air Force Academy, I have seen all aspects of an effective team. I later used those early experiences and lessons during a 16-year career in the NFL with the Denver Broncos, working my way up from a player personnel assistant to general manager of the team. The success that we had as a team, both on and off the field, reinforced my established beliefs in team building. As a team member, team leader, and team manager, I obtained this answer through my firsthand knowledge of the power of well-executed teamwork and what it can achieve for the individual members of the team and those affiliated with it.

Though teamwork is traditionally defined as selfless compliance with the needs of the group, today's team members require more individualized attention to bring out their maximum skills and production as effective members of the group. This requires new ways of selecting team members, training and developing team members, and motivating team members. The essential by-products of teamwork have not changed, and the strongest teams will be the most successful, but how you go about building and maintaining teams has changed. I have had the opportunity to build teams from a military perspective (where the accomplishment of the mission is not just vital, but life preserving) and through sports (college and professional), where end results are demanded, but personal relationships and personal development are also created. Working with team members who had three generations of influence and also had unique backgrounds and upbringing, I quickly learned that building a team requires patience, understanding, communication, and vision, to name just a few elements.

My goal is to bring you a perspective that very few have had the opportunity to experience. Success and failure at the team level are a constant, never-ending process that forces internal and external evaluation of team building and teamwork principles. Regardless of your industry or vocation, the techniques and ideas regarding teamwork that are given in this book will help you build a better team. These unique perspectives and new insights will fuel your ability and drive to mold and nurture a team at any level. These powerful tools will help you be a better team member, team leader, and team builder in any team effort while realizing the power of teamwork in its most successful forms and seeing how quickly teams can falter if they are not built on a firm foundation of well-thought-out plans and principles. By ultimately understanding the power of teamwork and what a team is capable of achieving, you will be able to organize a powerhouse of players that will accelerate and supercharge your business to reach levels of success you never thought possible.

Thank you for purchasing this book and investing your time in my experiences and stories. I came from humble beginnings, and I remain humbled by the teams I have been fortunate enough to be a part of. I hope this book helps you to build teams that will continue to inspire and motivate your personal endeavors because at the end of the day, we are only as strong as the pillars that support us.

Kindest regards,
Ted Sundquist

CHAPTER 1

THE TALENT: SPOTTING THE BEST AND THE BRIGHTEST

For any employer, manager, or business owner, the first step in the team-building process is to identify the best team members. If you have a limitless amount of cash flow, this can be very simple: just go to the best companies in the world and offer their leaders top dollar. You will get people whose résumés show proven success, and they will get raises, making everyone in the new company happy. However, we all know that in reality, money matters, and leaders have to work with limited resources when it comes to sculpting a team.

Even more important, just because someone is qualified for a position does not necessarily mean that he is the right fit. You would never hire a CEO with 20 years' experience to run your books, would you? And I can bet that you would never pay top dollar for an expert computer programmer to lead and implement strategic ideas in a new business, right? My point is that you have to find the right person for any position. It is not just about experience, résumé, credentials, or past success;

1

it is about finding a round peg for a round hole. As we move through this chapter, you will begin to understand exactly how to build the right team and spot the best talent at a discount. This means that while your competitors may not have seen the potential in an employee, you will be able to spot the diamond in the rough.

Spotting the talent is a tool that all great leaders understand. They have specific ways that they use to evaluate and screen candidates in order to locate the best and the brightest. This is not easy. In fact, it may be one of the hardest jobs any business owner will have to do. But the good news is there are insightful and helpful hints and resources out there that you can utilize in your own business.

The Fundamentals of a Team

During my time with the Denver Broncos, one of my greatest responsibilities was finding talent that other teams had passed over. It might be the young man with the questionable background but enormous potential, or the guy with poor collegiate statistics but great intangibles, or even the veteran whose skills were diminishing, but who still had hunger and a willingness to lead and mentor. Some teams would pass on these players, which made it easier for me to get them at a discount. But you should not take the plunge on these future employees without assessing them and ensuring that they fit your team's mold. Spotting the talent and building the team starts with understanding the team concept and exactly what your end result should look like. So before we dive into the basics of building a team, it is imperative that we first define a team, discuss the value of synergy, and talk about the importance of consistency. Only then will you have the fundamental principles necessary to begin designing the blueprint for your team.

Defining a Team

We often hear the word *team*, but we rarely think of its deepest significance. It has many meanings and, depending on the context, can include numerous different ideas and concepts based on who you are and where you came from. However, the basis for most of my life's work, as well as this book, is this word that we all know and this concept that we have all surely been a part of. Whether you are an employee, a family member, an athlete, a coach, a manager, a business owner, or anything and everything else, in essence, you are part of a team. A team is defined as two or more people combining their innate skills, abilities, and strengths to accomplish a goal or mission that would be unachievable by an individual.

Ed Roski is president and chairman of the board of Majestic Realty, one of the oldest and largest privately held real estate companies in the United States. He also is co-owner of the Los Angeles Kings and Lakers. Combining his love of sports with his passion for business, he is recognized as having played a critical role in developing the Staples Center, a landmark in downtown Los Angeles. Ed is also one of the Forbes 200 richest people in the United States. He takes an active role in the city's cultural and educational development, serving as chairman of the board of trustees at the University of Southern California and being on the boards of the Los Angeles County Museum of Art (LACMA), the Bowers Museum, the California

Science Center, the Natural History Museum of Los Angeles County, and the Los Angeles Sports and Entertainment Commission. In addition, he serves on the board of regents at Loyola High School and has joined the board of the National Geographic Society, serving on the executive committee. In 2007, he cofounded the Land of the Free Foundation to help veterans' families and now serves as its president.

He said, "Whether a team consists of two, five, ten, or hundreds of people, I always look to put together a team with complementary skill sets. It is very important to have individuals with varied outlooks, experiences, and abilities. I do not want all accountants or attorneys on my team trying to solve a problem. This practice compounds weaknesses and inhibits strengths. Too much familiarity and similarity prevents the team members from challenging one another, while stifling creativity. You have to search for a mixture of talent that complements each other."

Defining a team is about finding the best mix of people who will work together and nurture one another to promote growth and provide support. Many times, teamwork is about survival. Take nature, for example. In its simplest form, individuals in certain breeds of animals work together as members of a team in order to live. That is the goal and the mission. Without this teamwork imperative, an army of ants could not build an anthill, a swarm of bees could not create a beehive, and a pack of wolves could not hunt. Teamwork is the pursuit of survival and the quest for success.

Consider the example of a flock of geese. As the geese flap their wings, they create an uplift for the birds following. When they fly together in a V formation, the flock's flying range is 71 percent greater than that of any bird flying alone. Furthermore, when a goose falls out of formation, it suddenly feels the drag and resistance of trying to fly alone, and quickly gets back into the formation to take advantage of the lifting power of the birds in front. The geese in formation honk to encourage those up front to maintain their speed. When the lead goose gets tired, it rotates back into the formation and another goose flies out to the point position. When a goose gets sick or is wounded, two geese drop out of formation and follow it down to help and protect it. They stay with it until it either is able to fly again or dies. They then launch out on their own to find another formation or to catch up with the flock. These survival techniques are second nature to this flock of birds, but they also demonstrate a powerful example of teamwork and epitomize the definition of a team. The geese stand strong together, working to bring about a common goal, but also being aware that they are better able to do this if they simply stick together. This is the crux of any team.

My entire life's work has been dedicated to studying teams and building the best ones possible. But it all starts with understanding exactly what a team is, what a team does, and, ultimately, what a team is capable of. Michael Jordan once said, "Talent wins games, but teamwork wins championships." What kind of team do you want? One that peaks, or one that continues to climb? This book is about the climb, and that ascent starts with the synergy of your team.

The Synergy of a Team

The natural order of things suggests the survival of the fittest. Some achieve this through mutual coexistence and strength in numbers. However, the best and the brightest know that a team is the sum of its parts and that a group of people who actively focus on synergy will blow away the competition. Most people think that the bigger and stronger the team, the better equipped it will be to reach its goals, but in reality, the more interwoven and structured the team (independent of size) is, the greater the likelihood of consistent success. The team mentality is imperative for the team structure. A team uses its numbers to alleviate stress on an individual. No one person alone can accomplish what a team can, even with endless time and resources.

Vern Abila runs Abila Security & Investigations Inc., a high-profile and extraordinarily successful security company. Vern has developed a diverse client base that includes the U.S. government, Fortune 500 firms, private individuals, CEOs, and Hollywood megastars. Vern has personally consulted and/ or worked on a multitude of contracts, both domestic and international, providing security and vulnerability assessments, surveillance and countersurveillance operations, riot control tactics, overseas courier services, and private and corporate investigations, along with a wide variety of low- and high-threat protective details. Abila is considered a subject matter expert by the U.S. Department of State in VIP protection, critical infrastructure, and national leadership and diplomatic security for its Antiterrorism Assistance Program.

Abila has served on several high-profile, high-threat protective details for the U.S. Department of State. He received several letters of commendation from Ambassador Robert Frowick and other entities involved for his role in stopping an attack on the motorcade carrying Ambassador Frowick, Muslim-Croat federation president Kresimir Zubak and

Bosnian Muslim president Alija Izetbegovic. Needless to say, when Vern builds a team, it is truly a matter of life and death. The synergy of his team can save his client's life.

Vern told me the story of a time when he assembled a team of 50 agents for a corporate job overseas. He told his client that it would take two to three weeks to train the team. The corporation was concerned and wanted to know why the team members had not been previously trained. Vern explained to his megaclient that even though these team members came from backgrounds such as Delta Force, Navy SEALs, and Recon, it was essential that they take the time to mesh and ensure that the synergy was correct, because if it was not, they could fail. He assured his client that the individual team members were trained, but that they still needed to become a team.

When it comes to the group mentality, teamwork enhances the limited productivity of individuals in certain areas while maximizing it in areas in which the individual might otherwise excel. Coordinated efforts on a grand scale can suffocate an opponent or a problem by focusing the massive energy of a number of people, outmaneuvering the larger issues that a team may face. A strong team ensures stability and maintains the very survival of the group, which in turn usually leads to success, while also ensuring maximum efficiency in the use of resources (physical, intellectual, emotional, and so on). The sum of the parts can help strengthen even the weakest link, preventing one chink in the armor from causing the entire man to fall.

Good teams incorporate teamwork into their culture, creating the building blocks for success. Just look at the organizations in the NFL that have withstood rocky periods and maintained levels of excellence over the course of time.

They are capable of meeting challenges on and off the field as a result of the cohesiveness and synergy of their members. This creates stability in the face of crisis and is more apt to build long-term success, which is desired in both business and sports. In the business setting as well, synergy is a leading indicator and has a strong correlative relationship with how far a team can truly go. The idea of taking a group of different people from various backgrounds and intricately weaving them together to form a harmonious and congruent end result is the ultimate goal of any leader. So as we navigate this book, we will work together to not only understand the power of synergy, but also study and evaluate how to implement synergy in building and nourishing team efforts.

The Consistency of a Team

The basic essence of teamwork has never changed. For hundreds of years, the definition and concept of a team have remained consistent. The best teams are those that remain steady and dependable in their makeup, behavior, and results. Leaders of teams have to stay true to the definition and role of teamwork in achieving their goals and mission while being flexible in their techniques for building teams and motivating and developing their members. What works well with one group of individuals, in one environment, with one set of circumstances, influences, and dynamics won't necessarily work for another. However, there must be a fundamental consistency in your blueprint, morals, and overall mission. Great teams maintain predictability and rarely experience large swings one way or the other. In the business world, people want to work with and for teams that preserve a direct and straightforward approach to success.

Consistency is one part reliability and one part cohesion. Think about the most successful companies in the world— Coca-Cola, Apple, Microsoft, General Electric, Home Depot, and many others. While there are numerous differences among them, from product lines to advertising campaigns to upper management, these companies all have developed ways of producing an unwavering and steady consistency. It starts from their leaders and trickles down to the team as a whole.

Teams at Work 1: Creating the World's Largest Passenger Plane

Creating the world's largest passenger airplane is not a one-person job. In fact, it's not even a one-hundred-person job.

> Airbus began as a consortium of aerospace manufacturers [in France, Germany, and the United Kingdom in 1967]. Airbus employs around 63,000 workers at sixteen sites in four European Union countries.

There are subsidiaries in the United States, Japan, China, and India, with assembly facilities in France, Germany, Spain, and China. Manufacturing an Airbus airplane is literally a worldwide endeavor.

> [The signature aircraft of the Airbus family is] the A380, . . . a double-deck, wide-body, four-engine jet airliner. It is the world's largest passenger airliner and, due to its size, many airports have had to upgrade their facilities to properly accommodate it.

It is more than 250 feet long, weighs more than 500 tons, and can seat more than 550 passengers.

In 1988, a group of engineers began secret development of this ultra-high-capacity airliner.

> Major structural sections of the A380 are built in France, Germany, Spain, and the United Kingdom. Due to their size, traditional transportation methods proved unfeasible, so they [must be transported by unconventional means for final assembly in] Toulouse, France.

Building an airplane in different parts of the world to traverse different parts of the world is an especially daunting task. But through precision, planning, and amazing teamwork, Airbus accomplishes it dozens of times a year. After being assembled in France, the A380s are flown back to Germany where they are painted and outfitted. Using this process, Airbus is capable of producing four A380s per month. At the 2011 Paris Air Show, Airbus received total orders for 730 aircraft, valued at about $72.2 billion, setting a new record in the civil aviation industry. It takes hundreds of team members to build this aviation miracle, but the end result transports thousands of people across the world annually. Not even the most expensive machines could accomplish this amazing task. It can be carried out only through the synergy of an amazingly well trained and intelligent team working at full capacity. (Based on "Airbus" and "Airbus A380," *Wikipedia*, January 23, 2013, and January 27, 2013.)

A team is like a stock. There are many types of stocks, just as there are various types of teams. However, most investors look at stocks as being in two categories: low risk and high risk. Low-risk stocks are often referred to as "blue chips" and are generally consistent, with few price large swings. High-risk stocks can be those of start-ups and can see big jumps and big dips on a daily basis. You can make amazing amounts of money in these stocks, but you can also lose your entire portfolio. If you were investing all your money, where would you want to be? My guess is, in the comfort of the low-risk stocks. The same is true with teams. People do not want to work on teams with unpredictable swings. Sure, the team can hit a home run, but it may strike out plenty of times first. A team is only as good as it is consistent, and as we move forward in learning how to build the best team possible, remember that reliability is the backbone of any team.

That being said, let's begin to explore exactly how to spot the best and the brightest. As we move forward through these concepts, remember that understanding the definition of a team, the power of synergy, and the importance of consistency should be at the front of your mind.

Step 1: Blueprint Your Team

Before you interview the first candidate or read the first résumé, you have to create a blueprint for your team. I would surmise that you would not build a large home blindly. There's no way you would wing it. My guess is that you would have a detailed blueprint created by a qualified architect to bring this great project to fruition. Well, when it comes to building a team for your business, you are the qualified architect. It is your job and your responsibility. But the great news is that if you do a good job, you will reap the rewards from your informed and diligent efforts.

Dr. Charlie Palmer is known to most people as a smoke jumper. Smoke jumpers are wild-land firefighters who parachute into remote areas to fight wildfires. They are most often deployed to fight fires in areas that are extremely isolated. An exceptionally well-developed training program that has evolved over the course of more than 70 years mitigates the risks associated with this method of personnel deployment. The smoke jumpers are a highly skilled and intensely trained workforce that can be mobilized quickly for a myriad of work assignments in forestry, disaster relief, and emergency management.

He told me, "Smoke jumpers work off of a rotating list. Essentially, the U.S. government draws names out of a hat from its list of registered smoke jumpers. Less than 10 percent of the firefighters who apply to become smoke jumpers actually make it. It is of integral importance that the people selected are quality team members and meet the guidelines. Theoretically, two people who have never met each other could be deployed into a raging fire one day. If they cannot work together and were not properly screened for their skills and attributes, the end result could be disastrous." The U.S. government has a detailed list of qualifications and standards that potential candidates must meet before they are qualified to become smoke jumpers. The government follows its blueprint to the last detail when choosing team members because it is a matter of life and death.

In most major corporations or businesses, there is probably a well-oiled human resources department. Regardless, the people leading the team still have the responsibility for finding the best and the brightest. Whether the team involved is at a small business or a Fortune 500 company, the task is still the same; it's just more involved at the larger company. To start with, you should have a big-picture understanding of the current makeup of your team and the manner in which it is organized. Most companies already have some structures and teams in place; however, if you are a start-up, you may be attempting to assemble a team from day one. In any event, there is always a fluidity to team building. Sometimes you will be in a position to start the team from scratch, whereas other times you will have to rebuild a team, fill an empty spot, or even create a contingency plan in case one of your vital team members leaves.

Creating a strong blueprint will help you in times of need by keeping you one step ahead of situations that put teams into "crisis chaos." When you have already thought out your next personnel move if one is required, you are instantly ready to fill any and all positions to keep the team at peak efficiency. This also allows for an ongoing analysis of the talent available based on the skills that are being employed in a particular field. My hope is that when a crisis hits, you have already reviewed résumés and scouted your opposition and competitors; I also hope that even during successful periods, you are ready to upgrade your current membership to strengthen the team. You can see the types of individuals your competitors are after as well if names are pulled off your blueprint. Through your own evaluation system, you can view where your strengths and potential weaknesses are within the team, allowing you to move forward with the development or replacement of weaker members.

I carried my personal blueprint with me everywhere. It gave me a sense of what people were available, where they had been, where they were going, and any and all contact information and reports necessary to make a snap decision. For instance, in football, if there was an injury to a player on the road that required us to either fill the position immediately or look for potential short-term solutions, I could turn to my research and evaluations and instantly find replacements for team members, keeping the group focused on winning games and not worrying about the loss of talent.

So the question remains: how exactly should you develop a blueprint before you begin to build a team?

It Starts with Morals

The first thing any business owner should do in order to blueprint effectively for her team is to consider the type of moral fabric she would prefer to have in her team members. To me personally, morals are the glue that binds together the fabric of teamwork and what it's all about. You can build successful teams without regard to their internal makeup, but without some sort of guidance for behavior, there is certain to be instability. With instability come loss of production and ultimately failure to meet goals and missions. High morals allow for smooth interaction of team members (mentally and physically), keep undue pressures off the group, and allow for stability, which in turn creates long-term success.

For years the Broncos worked with an internalized code that was never formally stated. But the internalization of "the Bronco way" was accepted by all and created stability of interaction among departments within the organization. This stability held fast for years and brought the team much success. It wasn't until the club steered away from the Bronco way that things began to unravel. There was internal distrust and poor communication. The club lost its focus. This moral fissure came about because certain personnel hadn't been vetted in the proper manner and lacked an understanding of the teamwork culture that Denver had developed over years of success in pressure situations.

The ultimate goal is to find the correct "moral fits" for your company and avoid those that will lead to its untimely demise. This starts by evaluating the core set of values necessary to achieve the mission or goal at hand. Begin by asking yourself the following questions.

What Are the Purpose and Goals of My Company? It is vital to the success of your team that you define your purpose and the goals for your business. You should be able to answer this question in one or two sentences that clearly define the products or services that your company offers potential customers. Some companies are created to make money, while others are focused on philanthropy. Certain businesses work hard to create new products, while others try to improve on already existing ones.

Andrew Carnegie said, "Teamwork is the ability to work together toward a common vision. The ability to direct individual accomplishments toward organizational objectives. It is the fuel that allows common people to attain uncommon results." So from the get-go you have a responsibility to both yourself and your company to define a vision and push off the dock with an understanding of where you will guide the boat.

15

Your goals should be reflected in your morals, and your morals should be reflected in the goals you are looking to achieve. Every team has to set some moral standard concerning what it represents and the core characteristics to which it wants to implement its efforts. This is not to say that every team is required to have the highest moral standards and values at the forefront of all its labors, but those that do build this into their foundations based on their goals are more apt to have highly productive team members who contribute to the combined work of the group. The more productive and efficient this work is, the more likely it is that the group will achieve its goals. Lack of moral strength puts pressure on the team, both internally and externally, again stealing resources from the combined efforts.

This concept is best served when it is addressed at the beginning of any team effort, rather than being dealt with in the middle or as incidents occur. The Air Force Academy teaches its Honor Code to every incoming "doolie" (freshman) from the very minute he is sworn in as a cadet. This code is meant to be internalized (through instruction and implementation) to set a moral standard across all members of the Cadet Wing. Essentially, this code is a guiding light for the ultimate vision and goals of the Air Force. The service is clear on what it wants from its team members, and it tells them this from day one.

The code says: "We will not lie, steal or cheat, nor tolerate among us anyone who does." That's a pretty clear-cut, basic statement. But it ensures that everyone is working on the same page, level, and playing field, while also ensuring that all members of the team can depend on the words and actions of *every* member. Self-policing through the nontoleration clause brings some internal ownership. It's not easy, and it can be difficult for every individual, as well as for the group and the team. But this all starts with defining your goals for your company. The Air Force took a monumental step in making clear what it expected from its team members because it not only defined its personal goals, but also laid the foundation for every cadet and team member to come, which demonstrates the importance of understanding your own business's goals.

What Type of People Will Help Us Reach These Goals?   Business owners should understand the task at hand and the type of qualities that have proved successful in the past, all the while being mindful of the dynamics and differences in the present situation. For example, a certain situation might require a high-energy type of person rather than someone with a passive or sedate personality. Some situations might require brute strength rather than intellectual leverage. It really depends on the task and an understanding of the mindset needed to accomplish that task. It is up to you to make a list of the skills that you feel are vital to your company's success.

We have all heard the phrase "they can't all be choirboys" when describing the moral characteristics of some of the shadier team members. However, members must be able to trust that the other members are capable of producing under what are sure to be at times difficult and high-pressure circumstances. Those members who have shown a history of moral behavior are more likely to be able to be counted upon to perform at their maximum under pressure. Those who take moral shortcuts to accomplish their goals or carry out their roles within the group, or those who use those same shortcuts to override the goals or mission of the group for their own personal gain, don't fit the definition of what a team member is and therefore work against the combined efforts and have put their own interests not on a par with but above the interests of the group.

In the NFL, it is said that the best teams have the best locker rooms, and they do not mean mahogany cubicles and plush carpets. The best teams have players with high character and morals that permeate their preparations, both on and off the field. This moral compass keeps the group focused on the mission so that it tends to police itself from within and does not drain the resources of the organization or rely on upper-level management to keep it in line. Team members with high moral standards usually influence the group with strong leadership through their work ethic, example, and vocal guidance. True teams develop a strength that permeates from the inside out, meaning that they believe in the cause and will live and work by the standards necessary to accomplish that mission.

Finally, What Character and Moral Traits Do I Hold Close to My Heart?   Each of us has her own personal set of standards and guidelines by which she lives her life. My guess is that your company will be a reflection of who you are and what you stand for. Those individuals that you employ should have morals that mirror yours. Contemplate this list of morals as examples of those you can consider: wisdom, knowledge, courage, humanity, justice, hope, temperance, spirituality, forgiveness, humor, enthusiasm, curiosity, love of learning, perspective, open-mindedness, ingenuity, originality, kind-ness, honesty, generosity, leadership, and humility.

This is just a partial list, but it should give you a jumping-off point for the things you should consider when you are comparing your personal morals against those of future employees. Only you can decide which of these characteristics you consider to be nonnegotiable for you and your business and evaluate accordingly. Whatever the case, the most important piece of the equation is to have a list and use those intricate and well-thought-out traits to focus your search.

After answering these three questions, you should be able to plug these well-thought-out answers into your blueprint. So before you walk into the first interview, you are clear on the purpose of your company, the goals of your business, the types of people who will help you reach your goals, and the morals and character traits they will possess.

And Moves to Skills

Clearly, the first piece in developing a blueprint is building a foundation by understanding who you are and what your business looks like. The second part of the blueprinting process is evaluating and acknowledging the specific skill sets you desire in your employees.

An unknown author once said, "There are three types of workers: those who get things done, those who watch things get done, and those who wonder how so much got done." When you are evaluating the skill sets of potential employees, you have to decide what fits your need the best. We can all agree that we want the "doers," not the "sitters" or the "wonderers."

The best businesses are those that do not wait for direction, but find it themselves.

Only you can decide what is best for your team. You may want extremely hard workers, or you could prefer more balanced team members. Perhaps you prefer free thinkers, whereas another employer may desire people who take direction with ease. Whatever the case, this is your baby, and it is imperative that you consider what morals and character traits your employees must have.

When you are blueprinting, conventional definitions will tell you that the best team members put their own self-interest second to the needs and mission of the group. While that is true, it is also vital to consider that a strong individual can be a more valuable asset to the team than one who has been weakened by circumstances. Therefore, to me, among the more important aspects of team membership are self-awareness and maturity. The maturity brings experience and understanding, which, in turn, lead to self-awareness of one's capabilities and limitations and the ability to bring the two together to become a self-maximized component of the team.

Team members need to be willing to put the team's interests on a par with or above their own self-interest. Maturity allows for an understanding and willingness to put the team above oneself. Self-motivated individuals seem to blend best, as they tend not to drain resources away from other members of the team. They already have a firm understanding of the strengths that a team brings to attacking a situation, challenge, or problem, and they don't have to be reminded of the benefits of their own efforts toward achieving the goals.

Teams at Work 2: Get on the Pony Express

The Pony Express was a fast mail service crossing the Great Plains, the Rocky Mountains, and the High Sierra . . . from April 3, 1860, to October 1861. . . . This original fast mail "Pony Express" service had messages carried by horseback riders in staged relays to stations (with fresh horses and riders) across the prairies, plains, deserts, and mountains of the Western United States. During its 18 months of operation, it reduced the time for messages to travel between the Atlantic and Pacific coasts to about ten days, with telegraphic communication covering about half the distance across the continent and mounted couriers the rest.

William Russell, Alexander Majors and William Waddell were the three founders of the Pony Express. . . . [They] put [it] together in two months in the winter of 1860.

In a matter of sixty days, these three entrepreneurs reinvented the "postal service" at that time.

[This cutting-edge] undertaking involved 120 riders, 184 stations, 400 horses and several hundred personnel during January and February 1860. . . . The Pony Express demonstrated that a unified transcontinental system could be built and operated continuously year round. The route was divided up into five Divisions. . . . To maintain the rigid schedule, 157 relay stations were located from 5 to 25 miles apart as the terrain would allow for. At each *Swing Station* riders would exchange their tired mounts for fresh ones, while Home Stations provided room and board for the riders between runs.

This technique allowed the mail to be whisked across the continent in record time. . . .

The Pony Express had an estimated 80 riders that were in use at any one given time. In addition, there were also about 400 other employees including station keepers, stock tenders and route superintendents.

It's hard to think that there was a time when it took one 8.5 × 11 piece of paper upwards of ten days to reach its destination, but this was unconventional and record breaking at the time. Something that once had taken one man weeks and sometimes even months to accomplish was being achieved in less than 10 days by a well-trained team. In a time of war, turmoil, and the Wild West, those days could be the difference between life and death. (From "Pony Express Route Map Print," Zazzle.com, January 13, 2013, and "Pony Express," *Wikipedia*, January 25, 2013.)

Flexible individuals are also strong team members. They understand that every situation is fluid and that to a certain extent there will be unforeseen circumstances that will require quick changes in strategies and tactics and that will change their own roles within the team, perhaps both in the short and the long term. Team members of this type adapt readily and accept change, making them stronger contributors to the survival of the group. Those with a willingness to be trained, be taught, and study are more apt to realize their expanded abilities to contribute to the mission.

These are just a few examples of the types of skills you should consider. Every artisan has a set of abilities and qualities that enables him to become a master at what he produces. These abilities and qualities might be eyesight, dexterity, steady hands, intuition, balance, knowledge of materials, or something else. The task that is required of the individual is broken down into the elements required to execute that task and the mental and physical skills that the individual needs in order to execute those elements properly to complete the task. It all comes full circle. While this is not to say that someone should not attempt to execute a given task, her chances of achieving maximum standards and ultimate success are greatly reduced when she does not possess the full set of parameters.

In ancient times, the greatest archers had the keenest eyesight, steady hands, and controlled breathing. The best horsemen had high courage and a balanced body and were instinctively one with the mount. When blueprinting, you have to find your need and then search for the best piece to fill it.

The most efficient way of doing this is through a diagram box. Start by listing the positions on your team that you need to fill. This list can run horizontally on top of the box. These positions could be general manager, president, CEO, coordinator, vice president, head of advertising, director of marketing, and so on. Once you have this list, begin to fill the boxes with the specific skill set you would like candidates for these positions to possess. Next, decide what your budget for each candidate may be and insert those numbers into the corresponding box. Finally, shade each box with a color that corresponds to the value and need for the position in your company, with white being the first tier, gray the second, and black the third. Once this diagram is complete, it will be a handy reference sheet that you can use in all your interviews to attain a visual understanding of how your needs coincide with the skills of the candidate who is sitting in front of you at the time. Obviously, your needs may change over time, so always remember that this is a fluid process that requires constant attention and updating.

Take a look at this example:

	Left Tackle	Quarterback	Wide Receiver	Right Guard	Right Tackle
Starter	Tall, big, athletic ($1.5)	Smart, studious, athletic ($5.0)	Tall, good hands, quick ($3.5)	Good vision, big, strong leverage ($2.5)	Oversized, great blocker, tall ($4.0)

In this example, which I used while I was managing the Denver Broncos, I placed the position needs at the top. I would then shade each box according to need and placed in the box the skills required and the approximate amount of money I could spend on any position. This provided a valuable and easily referenced diagram that I could use during the hiring process.

In addition to creating a diagram box, when you are determining the skill sets you may need for your team, another effective tool is to study past team members and opponents who have excelled in the area you are considering. What were the skills they had that allowed them to fulfill the requirements of their position successfully at the highest standards or levels of production? In a sense, the leaders of the team are projecting the likelihood of the team member's producing at a high level through his proficiency at the individual components that are required for a given task. To decide what the necessary skills are, it is imperative that you understand and have a general knowledge of the task. You do not have to be an expert or personally have the ability to execute the position, but you should have a firm appreciation of how the position fits into the overall plan to reach the goal or mission.

For example, when I was the general manager for the Denver Broncos, we were known for our zone blocking system, which consistently produced running backs who would accumulate 1,000 yards each and every year. This went on for a long time as a result of the emergence of future Hall of Famer Terrell Davis. With this explosive talent, we quickly learned the type of skill set we desired for this position. By studying Terrell day in and day out, we used his performance as a prototype for future draft picks for the running back position. Thus, we used past success to predict future achievement, a skill that you can implement in your hiring techniques as a valuable resource to ensure that you get exactly the type of person you want to fill your company's needs.

It seems that putting together effective teams is even more challenging for businesses today because of the competition and the large pool from which to pick. Therefore, it is vital that the parameters be well thought out, become a consistent part of the selection process, and be strictly adhered to in ongoing evaluations. This makes for a more stable long-term relationship between the team members and the group, while also providing room for upward development and growth.

So what skills make for the best team members? That is a question that should be determined by the tasks required of the team members. There can be multiple tasks that contribute to the execution of a required undertaking. Depending on both internal and external influences, these requirements can all be standard among competitive teams, yet weighted differently based on the team's philosophy. For example, we all might agree that the CEO of a large business must have five distinct skills if she is to succeed, but those skills might be ranked in any number of ways depending upon the company's vision and goals.

However, the greatest gift I can give you from my experience in building and managing teams is the tips and tools that I used to spot the best and the brightest. It all starts with your understanding of the team game, but also deciding on exactly the type of person you are looking for with regard to morals and skills. We have spent the first part of this chapter designing your game plan; now it is time to implement it.

In its simplest form, you pick a team by reviewing the candidates' educational and employment history, confirming their prior achievements, speaking with past employers and coaches concerning how a candidate fits into the team concept, interviewing the individual, allowing current team members to come into contact with and give feedback on the candidate, watching the candidate's performance or behavior in team settings under other scenarios, and putting him through individual and team drills or simulations.

Almost every employer will take this commonsense approach to picking team members. However, the greatest managers and team builders acknowledge that there are unbelievably powerful skills that they can use to find the diamonds in the rough. Each team in the National Football League has an entire evaluation process that looks at prospective new members throughout each and every season. Not only are they evaluated on their past accomplishments at a lower level of play, like college, but they are compared and contrasted with the very elite of their incoming class. This evaluation process is based on a fundamental group of skills called the *critical factors*.

Step 2: Spotting the Talent

The critical factors are the core components of the makeup of the individual team member, regardless of his position or the tasks for which he is employed. These critical factors run vertically through the team and the organization. All members of the team should display the standard minimums in these areas. In football, these are the factors that are required to play the game and excel, regardless of position—things like character, athletic ability, mental alertness, competitiveness, and production.

The critical factors provide for longitudinal continuity in any group or organization. If you want a fast team, then you build speed throughout as a core component, which could become a critical factor. If you want a team that is active in the community and that rarely, if ever, creates problems away from work, you set character as a highly weighted critical factor. This gives the leadership flexibility to tweak the organization at times with regard to the mission requirements, but ensures that a minimum standard is maintained in various areas that are deemed essential to the identity of the team.

In the business world, companies will sometimes focus too much on the tasks required by the position to be filled and not on the core makeup of the team member filling the position. The job may be carried out, but the problems created by the individual as she executes that job will ultimately affect the other members of the team and hinder the achievement of the ultimate goal.

That being said, only candidates who meet the minimum requirements for your critical factors should be evaluated for open positions in your company. If they do not meet the standards of "who you are" as a business, then there is no reason to go forward with any further evaluation of their ability to execute the requirements.

Critical factors should be four to six elements that are at the core of the type of team member (not skilled position or job) that you want in your organization or group. For example, a football team may be drafting a quarterback. After hours of evaluation and assessment of inner needs and outer candidates, the team may decide to narrow its predetermined critical factors for its QB to athletic, intelligent, studious, quick learner, and multitasker. This list will allow the team to not only better acknowledge the type of candidate it is seeking, but also make quick decisions from a large pool of potential opportunities.

While the critical factors may change as the business world changes, the underlying concept remains exactly the same. Critical factors should be broken down into four distinct categories represented by the acronym TEAM.

T: Teamwork

A fundamental element of any team is its members' ability to work with one another to reach a common goal. Henry Ford once said, "Coming together is a beginning. Keeping together is progress. Working together is success." You can assemble the most talented group of people, but if they do not mesh well and are not capable of working together, it is all for nothing. Some people are leaders, while others happily receive direction. It is your responsibility at the beginning of the process to determine what type of team player you are searching for. However, it is vital that you include teamwork as your first critical factor because if you hire a candidate who is focused more on personal gain than on the team, he will not do you or your company any good.

Vern Abila told me, "When it comes to a team member, one in a hundred has something special that I look for. I use my own past experience and intuition to find the person that will work together and be a strong teammate."

When you are screening candidates, it is vital that you ask specific questions relating to teamwork and the candidates' experience with teams. I would always ask questions like:

Do you prefer to work in small groups, or do you work better on your own?

What is the greatest accomplishment you have had as a member of a team?

What is the largest group of people with which you have worked?

Do you hold strongly to your preconceptions, or do you listen to the opinions of others?

All these questions will help you determine what kind of team member you are interviewing, as not everyone enjoys playing a role in the synergy of a team. When considering teamwork, you also should pay attention to the candidate's ability to communicate. Communication is essential to team success, and if a team member does not interact well with others and offer positive opinions, while listening just as well, this will inevitably cause strain to the team dynamic.

Some critical factors that you should consider when focusing on teamwork are leadership, direction, communication, interactivity, listening, participation, team dynamic, coexistence, confidence, ego, and volunteering.

Each of these factors plays a direct role in a person's ability to be a valuable addition to a team. Depending on your vision and the setup of your company, some of these factors may be more important than others. It is ultimately up to you to understand your mission and find the best fit using these surefire evaluation techniques regarding teamwork.

E: Ethics

The second category of critical factors is a person's ethics. Potter Stewart once said, "Ethics is knowing the difference between what you have a right to do and what is right to do." Simply put, you want to hire people who will make the right decisions. When they don't, you open both your company and yourself to potential liability. Your employees are a representation of who you are and what your company is, and if they make unethical or immoral decisions, this can ultimately affect your reputation and your bottom line. You want to hire people who will do the right thing and, more important, will act without regard to their own best interest or gain.

Ethics can play a number of different roles when it comes to critical factors. In addition to the right versus wrong kind of ethics, you also have to determine what type of work ethic you want your employees to have. This may seem like an easy question to answer; after all, we all want hard workers. When it comes right down to it, however, it is vital to find potential employees who have balance. Hard work is great, but the last thing you want is to have a burned-out employee, as you will eventually find that your company is getting diminished returns from such a person. Quality of work can deteriorate if your employees are unhappy, so when you are interviewing, you should always determine the type of worker you are considering.

Some critical factors that you should consider when focusing on ethics are diligence, balance, work ethic, family life, hobbies, interests, honesty, sincerity, candor, bravery, and openness. These critical factors will make a large difference in the type of employee you will eventually hire. Screening résumés and interviews with these factors in mind will help you decipher the longevity and dedication that a candidate will have with regard to your company. Having to train and incorporate new employees costs valuable time and money, so it is imperative to your success and the mentality of your company that you eliminate turnover and replacements. By understanding a candidate's ethical obligations and fortitude on the front end, you can prevent lost time and money.

A: Attitude

Everyone has an attitude. Some people have a positive one, while others tend to focus on the negative. The team's mentality and ultimately its performance will often be defined by the overall attitude that is injected into it. When interviewing for open positions in your company, you should consider people's attitude, as it will almost certainly be an indicator of their overall behavior and performance. In the business setting, there are deadlines, obstacles, stress, and numerous challenges that can unexpectedly present themselves. If you sense an issue with a candidate's attitude during an interview, imagine how that attitude will present itself when the going gets tough. When things are bad, the negative will be magnified.

Ed Roski, billionaire and CEO of Majestic Realty, told me that when it comes to a team member's attitude, there is no substitute for enthusiasm. Ed looks for people who are very enthusiastic and are comfortable with challenges. At this level, most candidates have already been vetted for their competence and their ability in their area of expertise. As a visionary, he wants people who will take on a particular project as their own, who live and breathe the challenges of the task and make it a part of themselves to solve the problems and complete the project. He says there are people who can do a "decent" or a "good" job for you, but he is looking beyond that. You cannot take individuals with basic skills or knowledge in an area and just throw them into certain high-level business situations, as that is a recipe for failure. You need to have a solid understanding of the necessary dynamics of a project and task in order to accomplish it. Then you can attack it with vigor and enthusiasm.

Within a team, each and every participant plays a distinct and valuable role. Consider a doctor's office, for example. There are secretaries who answer the phone and schedule appointments. Then there are receptionists who meet the patients and sign them in. Next, the patients will meet with nurses, who will do a prescreening and gather information before the doctor sees them. And finally, the patients will interact with the doctor and be diagnosed or evaluated. At any point in this intricately woven team, one person with a bad attitude can spoil the entire experience. When one employee has a negative approach to dealing with a patient, the damage is done. When you are hiring for your team, you have to study and evaluate the demeanor and attitude of people before you offer them the job.

At times people put their best foot forward in an interview, but then become complacent and resentful when they have the position. You should ask a number of questions and not be afraid to challenge job applicants with theoretical situations to see how they would react. They can fool you for only so long. As you familiarize yourself with candidates, you will know which ones have a positive attitude and which ones do not. Consider their facial expressions, their dress, and the manner in which they speak, act, and sit. These nonverbal clues can tell you a lot about their attitude. Do not leave any stone unturned when it comes to your job applicants. Small intricacies can make a huge difference in the success or failure of your company.

Some critical factors that you should consider when focusing on attitude are facial expressions, dress, demeanor, approach, manner, outlook, thoughts, feelings, opinions, point of view, and posture.

M: Mind

The final category of critical factors that you should consider when looking for talent is the mindset of the candidates that are in front of you. In my opinion, the strength of your employees' minds will be the most important indicator of their ability to reach high levels of success. The greatest thinkers always lead the most accomplished companies. When we refer to the mind, we are not just talking about intellect and intelligence, but also about vital factors like creativity, focus, and strength.

When you have a group of people working together who have the same mindset, your company will be able to move mountains. Buddha once said, "The mind is everything. What you think you become." When you are interviewing, you should focus your time and energy on those people who will truly spend their time thinking for your company—thinking about how to improve it, how it can reach new levels of success, and how to streamline the team mentality. There is a lost art of thought, and few people really spend the time necessary to focus on the task at hand and work meticulously to complete it.

The mind is a powerful tool that can be filled with information and resources. When you find a team member who is willing to fill her mind with your vision and goals, you will quickly see results. The ability to multitask, put out fires, alleviate stress on the entire team, and come up with helpful and useful solutions to problems all come from thought and the mind.

Some critical factors you should consider when focusing on the mind are intellect, studiousness, focus, creativity, strength, brainpower, cleverness, quick-mindedness, being solution-oriented, multitasking, and experience.

The TEAM acronym is a vital tool for categorizing potential applicants. Building a team is an intricate responsibility, and having a game plan for executing this task can often make the difference between building a team that is successful and building one that has enormous limitations. However, I am a strong proponent of cross-checking and leaning on your current resources and team members to ensure that your decisions and instincts are correct. The next section will help you determine whether you have made the best decisions for your future team by cross-checking to ensure that you avoid the wrong type of team member.

Step 3: Dodging the Busts

Two heads are better than one not just when you are a team, but also when you are picking a team. In the NFL, we had only a limited number of draft picks through which to assemble the greatest team possible. Each one of these draft picks had enormous value. If we evaluated them correctly, we could pick a team member who could essentially turn around our franchise. However, if we missed on a player, we would waste a valuable resource. To "dodge the bust," we would ask for the opinions of others and cross-check references and players' backgrounds to ensure that we were picking wisely.

The same is true in business. When you hire a new team member, you are making an investment. It will take time, money, and resources to develop the new asset. You will have to train your new team member, spending valuable staff time and person-hours to bring her up to speed. After investing this time and money in your new hire, if the relationship ultimately does not end well, you have wasted part of your business's resources.

There are surefire tools and means that you can use to ensure that your hires are going to be a part of your business over the long run.

Cross-Checking

One of the essential ways to predict the likelihood of your new employees' success is to constantly seek out multiple opinions and input. I call this cross-checking. In any interview, you will certainly have an instinctive reaction to the person you are meeting. However, you should compare your gut response with the feelings of others. When interviewing new players, we would always have what seemed like an entire team of our own in the room. This helped to prevent us from being fooled by smoke and mirrors. Sometimes people simply connect. It can skew your opinions and evoke emotions that really have nothing to do with the interviewing process.

Teams at Work 3: The Trans-Alaska Pipeline System

The Trans-Alaska Pipeline System (TAPS) [is one of the world's largest pipeline systems. It] includes . . . 11 pump stations, several hundred miles of feeder pipelines, and the Valdez Marine Terminal.

Built over the course of three years in the late 1970s and crossing 34 major rivers and 800 streams, it was the answer to the sharp rise in oil prices in the United States. The team that built the pipeline had to address a wide range of difficulties. Most of these challenges stemmed from the horrible terrain and weather conditions. Simply put, it was extremely cold and extremely isolated.

> The construction of the pipeline was one of the first large-scale projects to deal with problems caused by permafrost, and special construction techniques had to be developed to cope with the frozen ground. The project attracted tens of thousands of workers to Alaska, causing a boomtown atmosphere in Valdez, Fairbanks, and Anchorage.

Workers were constantly required to implement quick and effective solutions to unforeseen problems created by the weather and the terrain. They had to think on their feet to meet deadlines and avoid setbacks.

> More than $8 billion was spent to build the 800 miles of pipeline. The construction effort also had a human toll, as 32 employees died from causes directly related to the construction. The pipeline is checked on and evaluated on a daily basis to prevent leakage and other serious issues. These external inspections are only part of standard maintenance. Machines are used to check the pipelines for correct flow and maximum efficiency. In 2010 alone, 226,174,050 barrels moved through these pipelines. In fact, more than 10 percent of all the oil produced in the United States is transported by the Trans-Alaska Pipeline System. Hundreds of team members have the job of ensuring the stability and consistency of the pipeline system, even spending almost two consecutive days fixing a bullet hole in the pipe in 2001. (From "Trans-Alaska Pipeline System," *Wikipedia*, January 17, 2013.)

For example, let's say you are interviewing a potential candidate for an open position in your company. The young woman sitting in front of you was referred to you by a family friend and actually attended the same college as you. From the first handshake, you are already biased in one direction. You feel a responsibility to your friend, but you also love the idea that the two of you can exchange stories about the University of Wherever. However, suppose that, at the end of the day, this candidate is not the right fit for your position. She could be underqualified, be overqualified, or lack the correct team mentality. Nonetheless, you offer her the job because you connected with her. Now, I am not saying that there is no value in that connection; I am just saying that if there were five other people in the room along with the two of you, they could tell in a minute that she was not the right fit.

Dr. Charlie Palmer, a well-known smoke jumper, told me, "When picking a team, I rely heavily on trustworthy evaluations from other supervisors at work, and any direct contact former employers had with the potential candidate. I do not settle for my own mind, heart, and two eyes. Just as we attack wildfires in teams, we choose our jumpers in teams."

I always say that every interview deserves the attention of at least six eyes. That means that whenever you are hiring a new person, you should have at least two other employees in the room to offer opinions and cross-check your ultimate conclusions about each candidate. This will help eliminate personal bias or weighted individual evaluation by a single decision maker. It allows for multiple opinions given a set of standard criteria, but viewed under different circumstances, at different points in time, and under different environmental influences.

Look Outside

Another tool you should consider implementing in your hiring system is looking outside the box. Consider bringing in outside consultants who are familiar with the requirements of various positions within your business. Their perspective will be a bit more generic, but still within the realm of understanding the goals and the mission at hand. It will also take all emotion out of the decision. When you are hiring for your company, it is only natural for you to have your heart in the process. This is your baby, and each and every decision is a big one for you. But it should not be. Building a team is a systematic and unemotional experience, or at least it should be. When your heart gets involved, your instincts will become muddled and ineffective.

By hiring a human resources company to help you build a team, you take the process out of your own hands. Obviously you will play a role in the overall decision-making process, but sometimes limiting that role can be advantageous to the overall success of a team. When you hire someone, you are invested both in him and in his success. That investment can end up being a good one or a bad one. When it is a good one, everybody is happy. But when it turns sour, you have to be able to cut yourself off from the problem and get rid of the bad milk. When you do not have an immediate emotional involvement with your team members, this task will become much easier.

Review Your Blueprint

Another way to avoid the pitfalls of making a poor addition to your team is by reviewing the blueprint you created before you began interviews. This can be done through a thorough development of the initial evaluation and hiring process. You need to know full well who you want to be as a team, recognize what you are trying to accomplish in terms of your goals and your mission, understand the requirements for accomplishing that mission at a high level of excellence, dissect the components of executing the various required tasks to reach those goals or accomplish that mission, and weight those that are most important to your team if it is to achieve the requirements and reach the stated goal.

Your blueprint is your personal mission statement for your company. It tells you exactly what you wanted to achieve when you began it. As your company grows and your teams multiply and divide, it can be easy to lose sight of what is important. We hear time and time again of companies that reinvent themselves and go back to their roots. Over the years, they have simply lost their vision and fallen off track. The more employees you have, the greater the challenge of staying on course will be. You will be pushed and pulled in many different directions, but ultimately you created your business for a purpose, and you should never deviate from that standard.

Reviewing your blueprint will help you make wise and directed hiring decisions to execute the goals you have for your business. You do not want to get lost in the glitz and glamour of high-profile team members if that was never part of your destiny. In the NFL, there are numerous teams that focus on character when they are assembling players. They never deviate from that standard. No matter how talented a player may be, if that player carries unnecessary baggage or questionable morals, they will politely pass on him. That is because they stay linked to their blueprint. If and when they deviate from this practice, they will waste valuable time and resources, and will ultimately find out that it was never worth the risk. By remembering who you are and building your team to mirror that image, you will ensure that you do not take unnecessary risks, and you will avoid the bad apples.

Evaluate Long; Study Hard

Although taking more time to study and evaluate potential job candidates would seem like common sense, most employers spend only a small amount of time doing so. When you are hiring and building a team, a résumé and an interview are simply not enough to let you avoid bad decisions. If you put in the work and still hire a bad candidate, so be it. But do not ever be part of the majority that makes poor team-building decisions because of a lack of effort in the process. I have known employers to pass on a job applicant because there is a misspelled word on her résumé or to say no thank you when a candidate is not dressed properly for an interview, and we have all heard of the executive who crumples up a piece of paper and places it on the ground to see if the applicant will throw it away as he walks by it.

Returning to Vern Abila and his world-renowned security company, he told me, "When assembling a team, the first impression makes all the difference. How people walk into my office can be a make or break for me. What they wear, their body language, and how they address my colleagues and me often predicts the kind of team member they will be. I can tell in the first five minutes if this is a guy who has what it takes to be placed in a high-stress environment and save someone's life."

If you spend time creating a cohesive and well-planned interview process, you will be in a better position to dodge the busts. In today's world, there are endless resources at your fingertips through the Internet. Make it a point to cross-check résumés against the web and social media sites. I have heard time and time again of employers finding out that team members are actually habitual drug users or even have a criminal history just by checking their social media sites.

Furthermore, always ask for references and check on the references that candidates provide. You can tell a lot about potential team members based on what previous employers, friends, or mentors are willing to say about them. Consider whether these statements are genuine, and do not be afraid to push those references by asking tough questions about the person whom you recently interviewed.

Finally, take the time to compare the skills and attributes of your potential team member to those of former team members. If one of your most valuable employees has just departed for a new job and you have to fill the vacant spot, consider what it was about that departed employee that made her such a good fit with the team dynamic. Then, when you are interviewing people, see if you can discover a similar set of skills. This practice is extremely useful as you use past performance to predict future results.

When it comes down to it, the last thing you ever want to do is to build a team that is destined for failure. Narcissistic individuals, individuals who haven't worked in a team setting and are uncomfortable doing so, those who lack the capability to see and understand the big picture, those who fail to do timely work, unorganized individuals, inflexible individuals, those who place their own self-interest above and not equal to or below the needs of the team, individuals who don't like a structured chain of command, and those who don't like to compete and rely on others' efforts in determining the outcome of their own are all people that you should avoid like the plague.

To truly test its capacity, a team inherently has to go through significant pressure situations in order to realize its own capabilities. You can assemble the very best and brightest talent available, all with outstanding qualifications and past accomplishments. You can assemble a team for a clear-cut cause, define the goals, and establish the mission. All of the requirements for assembling a good team can be fulfilled, but until the team members face a challenge together head on and overcome adversity in doing so, they may never realize their full potential as a group.

In 1980, Ken Hatfield was in his second season as head coach of the Air Force Academy. He realized that if his team was to compete in the Western Athletic Conference, he was going to have to find a system that would allow him to recruit talent that met the standards of the academy and maximized its strengths of discipline and intelligence. Because of its high academic standards, the academy was limited in the types of students and players it could put on the field. However, Coach Hatfield introduced the wishbone offense, recruited heavily out

43

of Texas and California, then made the commitment to implement this new offensive system and employ numerous freshmen on his varsity team. The result was a 2–9–1 record the first year.

Hatfield's Falcons were clearly overmatched by their opponents, and the offense was too complicated and required too much coordination to execute effectively that first year. The team fumbled an enormous amount, players ran in the wrong direction, and the timing looked nothing like the well-oiled machines of Texas and Oklahoma in the 1960s and early 1970s. But the coaching staff stayed committed to this young group, which grew together both as cadets and as football players.

The second season saw glimpses of success and the emergence of some rising stars from this young group of players. The season ended with a trip to Japan to play in a game known as the Mirage Bowl. Air Force faced San Diego State in what should have been a blowout by the Aztecs. The Falcons had won only three games all season, had traveled almost 5,800 miles to play their last game, and were heavy underdogs. Something clicked that evening for a group of young cadets, while their coaches and their program were looking to build an identity on the other side of the world. The Falcons defeated San Diego State in a game that would establish the class of 1984's confidence in what Ken Hatfield and his staff were trying to accomplish. The result was a 4–7 record.

Leaders both on and off the field stepped forward, and the following year Air Force won the Commander-in-Chief's Trophy for the first time in the history of the school, defeated Notre Dame for the first time in its history, beat perennial conference champion BYU in Provo, Utah, then went on to win its first ever bowl game against Vanderbilt. The final record was 8–5.

The next season, the class of 1984 took the lessons learned over those prior three seasons and built a 10–2 record, with 8 straight wins, a victory over Notre Dame, wins over Army and Navy for the Commander-in-Chief's Trophy a second time, and a final victory over Ole Miss in the Independence Bowl to finish ranked thirteenth in the nation. Without the early pressure and pitfalls, the sting of failure, and the group's continued efforts to achieve success, this class would not have seen a turnaround from 2–9–1 to 10–2 in only four years.

What people do not know is that the culmination of this unbelievably successful team had started five to seven years earlier, when Coach Hatfield and his assistant coaches were watching game films of these young men's high school performance. They were interviewing them extensively and evaluating their character and morals. They had blueprinted, cross-checked, and meticulously studied every facet of their inner makeup. Coach Hatfield and his staff strategically and intelligently built a successful team. When a team reaches its goals, it is almost clockwork that you can turn the hands of time back and see exactly where this success came to fruition. It all started with finding the best and the brightest.

After reading this chapter, you should now have crucial tools and resources that will help you pick a team that can move mountains. Doing so is not overly complicated, but it does require hard work, dedication to the process, and self-control. Removing your emotions, eliminating your ego, and making tough decisions based on proven data can make the difference between your team's reaching the moon or falling short of the stars.

CHAPTER 2

THE MISSION: FUDES FOR THOUGHT

After reading the first chapter of this book, you should have a thorough and crystal clear understanding of how to hire the best and the brightest that your industry has to offer. This is not an easy task, as the hiring pools are large, and most employers can dedicate only a limited amount of resources to the process. However, with careful planning and appropriate know-how, you can traverse the rough terrain and find those special individuals who can truly make a difference to both you and your company.

But hiring these integral pieces is just the beginning. Shortly after bringing new employees on board, your focus must shift toward integrating them and folding them into your existing organization. This occurs through a number of different venues and mediums, but it really kicks off with educating individuals about your organization's vision. Think of this as being like the chorus to a hit music song. It is the heart of everything and really the driving force behind your company's ultimate goals.

When you find people who want to be part of a team, you can then shift their spirits and desires to something that you can channel to success. When speaking about the power and intricacies of a team, Ed Roski talked about building the Staples Center, home of the Los Angeles Lakers:

> *My experience is that these megaprojects can only happen with a clear mission and a team to execute it. No individual or small group of individuals can accomplish something like that. It really takes a full-on team. It takes specialists in different areas that can accomplish something by combining all their different talents. It is always interesting to see how the team develops and takes on a personality all its own by combining all the different disciplines. It is amazing to me how you can take an architect from New York and a designer from New Orleans, throw in a couple of bankers from New York and insurance companies from the Midwest, and then ask all of these different people to become a team. Individually they're really good, but by combining them and putting a team together, then you can really get something going that actually works. Everybody changes a bit when they become a team member. All of a sudden they're relying on the guy on the left and on the right. As opposed to just relying on their own staff and office, they're forced to rely on others for it to succeed.*

Mahatma Gandhi once said, "A small body of determined spirits fired by an unquenchable faith in their mission can alter the course of history." Each and every business around wants to be the one that shapes its industry, changes the game, and raises the bar. Each wants to be the one that alters the "then" and defines the "now." But it takes a strong workforce with a clear and concise understanding of your mantra—your mission. This truly begins with your defining and creating a mission statement to represent the dream and foresight of your company's goals.

Stating Your Mission

There are plenty of definitions of a mission statement, but for the purposes of this book, let's consider the mission statement to be the all-encompassing understanding of why a team exists in the first place. It could be to win games, create a good product, offer a needed service, raise money in a philanthropic manner, or even just have a good time. It can be serious or not so serious, but for the sake of our conversation and in the realm of business, let's assume that a team's mission is twofold: to survive and to succeed.

We often see the fight for survival in its purest form in nature and the endurance of a species. Everything that takes place, such as migration, shelter, reproduction, fight or flight, predation, and so on, is done to ensure that the individual animal and the family will survive and thrive, in order to procreate and renew themselves time and time again. While some of this behavior is voluntary, other parts of it are involuntary and driven by internalized instincts.

The outside forces of nature continually both help and hinder this process. But to overcome these forces, most species will evolve and augment their strengths to ensure that, at the very least, a significant number of the strongest members will live and reproduce.

The human situation is no different. Because teams and organizations can be brought together for various goals and objectives, it important to clearly define what the desired outcome may be and how the team should go about achieving it.

The second part of any team's mission is attaining the greatest amount of success, both individually and as a complete unit. This is where things can get a touch more involved. Success has many definitions and, depending on the industry and the type of organization that you are a part of, can take many different forms. Despite this, all companies should create a mission statement indicating what they want to accomplish.

In fact, when I was interviewing Ed Roski, he told me, "In my own company, I've never really thought of a formalized mission statement. No kidding. We've been in business since 1948 and in a privately held company throughout the United States. I just never really thought about formalizing it until we spoke. I fully understand the importance of it, and I thought, 'Heck, I should sit down and draft up a real mission statement,' . . . At least to have everybody look at it and contemplate it. We don't have a formal one, but we may have an understanding of what our focus is in business and how we go about accomplishing it."

Whether your company is new or old, successful or on a pathway to improvement, there is always the need to create a mission statement. This chapter will help you and your company not only build a meaningful mission statement, but also create the structure to implement it within the everyday fabric of your business.

The Value of a Mission Statement

The value of a well-thought-out and well-defined mission statement cannot be overstated. A mission statement is like a lighthouse for a boat at sea. It is a guiding landmark that draws people in and offers them direction and purpose. Without it, your organization and its employees would simply be lost in the ocean of objectives.

A mission statement allows you to work both with and against outside forces. It lets you use the winds and waves to reach your next port, to put you in more fertile waters and reap the harvest, or to race across the water at speeds that would otherwise be unattainable.

A mission statement accomplishes the following crucial goals for an organization.

> *It outlines objectives.* Objectives are like points on a map that connect your path from beginning to end. If you fail to reach the first point, it becomes increasingly difficult for you to reach the second, and so on. A firm understanding of the components required on the journey toward mission completion will easily lead you to outline the necessary objectives, goals, or benchmarks that are vital to reaching your team's stated calling.

> *It prevents waste.* Creating a mission statement helps in the efficient use of energy and resources, both of which are finite for every team or organization. Whether we are talking about skilled employees, financial assets, time, or anything else, if the team knows its ultimate

purpose, it should by the very nature of things expend those resources efficiently in a fashion that will enable it to accomplish the mission.

It keeps people focused. In a perfect world, employees would be free from all sorts of outside forces and influence. However, there are hundreds of distractions that can pull your new hires in many different directions. A direct mission statement points everyone along the same path, channels both mental and physical energy toward the stated purpose and goal, provides clarity of effort, and can emphasize the importance of the need for mutual effort by accentuating the sheer size of the task at hand, all the while highlighting the notion that without teamwork, the goal simply cannot be accomplished.

By keeping these three reasons for the value of a mission statement at the front of your mind while actually building the underlying objective, you will find yourself better equipped to create a guiding light that will both benefit and represent your company's vision.

Yet the starting point for all these elements is to firmly define your mission. If you do not do so, you're a ship without a rudder, floating aimlessly on a sea that randomly takes you wherever the wind blows. The boat stays afloat, and the team might survive, but you don't get anywhere, no matter how strong the wind may be. Resources dry up (food, water, and perhaps shelter from the elements), and you eventually wither away and die. Or the team members just split up and go their own way.

Building a Mission Statement

Now that you are clear on the value of a mission statement, it is time for you to begin building one for your business. When I was the general manager for the Denver Broncos, I had the responsibility for bringing an unbelievably different group of people with various personalities together as one.

That being said, the way to build a mission statement is by taking the following crucial steps.

Start with the End in Mind

The best way to begin this job is to start with the end in mind. Every journey has an eventual destination. This is not necessarily what many people on the outside might expect, either. Start by finding the end purpose. As easy as this sounds, it can be the most difficult part of the process.

You have to answer questions like: Why do we exist in the first place? What is our ultimate accomplishment? Is there an end point, or do we evolve?

For example, in football, the outwardly understood "mission" is to win football games. The very definition of the game itself is to score as many points as possible in a given time frame and to prevent your opponent from doing the same — a pretty easy outward interpretation of the purpose of a football team.

However, consider the game of football from a young child's perspective as he advances both in age and in level of play.

At the Pee Wee level, the mission might be more to teach the fundamentals of the game and to foster within the players an enthusiasm for participating in the sport, now and in the future. Coaches focus on unity, competitive balance, and communication.

At the high school and college level, the mission might be to teach the principles of teamwork, physical fitness, and individual growth (mental and physical) as part of the greater educational process.

Finally, at the professional level, the mission becomes providing a source of entertainment that encourages the public to want to affiliate with the team and the sport and, by doing so, spend money in support of this affiliation (buy tickets and apparel, support other products affiliated with pro football, and so on). Ultimately, though, it is about winning and working as a successful business.

Through reviewing the development of the football life cycle, it should be clear that an organization's mission is not always what it appears to be on the surface. The end result is often intricately thought out and enormously different from what first meets the eye. So, while outwardly it remains obvious that you play the game to win the game, inwardly there can be an entirely different agenda.

The same will prove true in your industry. In the business world, the outward interpretation is to make money. It's the scorecard for capitalism. You need to use your resources in the most efficient manner possible in order to survive and succeed in the "economic jungle."

The owner, leader, CEO, or board of directors can have an internal mission statement that points away from making money and more toward philanthropic accomplishment, maximized growth, individual development, or something else.

Again, the list of missions is as big as imagination and vision will allow.

Ask yourself and your company: what is the goal of this business? Once you can answer this question, you should have a clear understanding of the endgame and then begin to move to the next vital piece of developing your mission.

Be Flexible

Regardless of the destination (make money, win, reach point B, or whatever), the basic steps in achieving that result are the same regardless of vocation, industry, or external forces. Missions can be long-term or short-term. They can evolve and grow as the team does, or they can remain static and constant to ensure continuous production and survival. Whatever the case may be, when you are contemplating a mission statement, approach it with an understanding that as your goals change, so does your mission statement. You have to be flexible.

In the jewelry business, people know that you can take a beautiful ring and resize it if it is made of silver. It is not easy, but it can be done. However, every jeweler knows that you can never resize something made of platinum. Thus, your mission statement should be written in silver, not platinum. It should be meaningful and should rarely change, but if the need arises, it should be capable of shifting and being reshaped. You always want to be tied to your goals, but also flexible enough to welcome change. Never let your biased view of your objectives prevent you from taking an opportunity to grow.

The Culture Should Reflect the Mission

Those who are setting out to define the purpose of their organization or team should take into account exactly what it is they are ultimately trying to accomplish through their efforts and include in it an understanding of the cultural tone with which they hope to go about accomplishing that mission.

If you create a mission and make a promise to new team members that is not reflected in the inner culture of the company, you will often find this disconnect and issues with new employees reflected in your business practices.

Ed Roski, president of Majestic Realty, talked to me about the importance of culture. He said, "Most companies develop their own culture depending upon the individuals in the company in a direction that they are personally interested in going, and probably in some way you attract people that are somewhat similar to your ideas and concepts of the benefits of living in America and where we want to go with what we want to contribute."

It is important that you emphasize the values and/or core characteristics that you want to internalize within your team and that you want to be recognized and defined by others outside the boundaries of membership. Your mission and your culture must go hand in hand as mirror images of each other.

Take a Broad but Detailed Approach

Staying broad at the top and narrowing as you move toward the details is imperative as you establish a usable mission statement. Giving both your employees and the consumers a general description of your goals combined with a detailed description of how those objectives will be reached will help top executives' visions become a reality through employee action.

Furthermore, taking a broad approach allows for flexibility and continued growth as a team. If you fail to accomplish your overall mission in a given year, your efforts can still be directed toward doing so the following year because you are not so detail-oriented on the front end. If you paint yourself into a corner with a particular mission statement and then fail to achieve your end goal, your company may experience a sense of failure.

Stand firm on what you want to accomplish and go into detail in your plans and procedures, but leave room for inter-mediate goals to mark your way along the journey. You can always change your route to your destination. You can get there early, or you can be a few days late. You can start out fast and slow down to conserve fuel. There might some unplanned stops for sightseeing or for maintenance and repairs.

But ultimately, your final destination doesn't change. Your goal is to get from point A to point B in a manner that uses the personnel and resources at your disposal most effi-ciently, conducted by using the core concepts and fundamen-tal values on which your company is built.

Ready to Go?

With these careful considerations regarding your approach to a mission statement in mind, the next step is to actually begin conceiving one. The foundation has been laid, and the bricks and mortar are sitting on the land. It is time to start building the house. Consider your organization's culture in planning your mission statement by listing all the adjectives you feel you would want others to use to describe your efforts and endeavors. Narrow your list down to no more than five strong and representative words. Then do the same with tangible concepts that are vital to reaching the goals and carrying out the mission of the team and the organization. Narrow this list down as well to no more than five specific and relevant adjectives.

Now, using the end as your beginning, take your carefully thought-out concepts and the adjectives that you hope are used to describe how you go about attaining them, and craft a two- to three-sentence statement that any and all objectives, operations, and efforts could be filtered through. This should be succinct, focused, clear, and well thought out. Less is more when formulating a mission statement, although detail and clarity are required. The mission statement should have only one end, and up to five core concepts to get there. The end should be broad, and the core concepts should be narrowly tailored.

For example, consider the mission of one of my favorites, the U.S. Air Force Academy:

> **The Air Force Academy Mission** *is to educate, train and inspire men and women to become officers of character, motivated to lead the United States Air Force in service to our nation.*

Taking this even further, I would imagine an NFL team's mission statement would sound something like this:

> *The mission of the Denver Broncos is to win the Super Bowl by channeling all our efforts through focused determination,*

unity of effort, detailed direction, and excellence in execu-
tion that culminate in success both on and off the field.

In this example, the broad goal is to win the Super Bowl and achieve success both on and off the field. The narrow objectives detail how this will be accomplished, seemingly through determination, effort, direction, and execution.

Whether the specific organization is involved in football, journalism, security, education, politics, or any of thousands of other industries, the principles that lead the organization to strength through numbers are fundamentally the same, regardless of the mission.

Many companies are started with an individual's goal in mind. It usually emanates from the founder, the CEO, or some other leader. Generally speaking, the top person's objective is to have others judge him to be the best at doing a particular thing.

As difficult as it can be to create a mission for your team, it eventually becomes clear-cut when you remove emotions and concentrate solely on the task. A mission encompasses the entire organization—all aspects, every facet, every member, every piece of equipment, and all the energy and time that are expended.

When I was general manager of the Denver Broncos, the team's mission was to win Super Bowl championships. Teams were built, torn down, and then built up again. Players were hired, coaches were fired, money was spent, meetings were conducted, and enormous amounts of attention were dedicated to practicing and perfecting skills. All of these came together with the goal of winning a Super Bowl. And we did—twice, in fact. Even more special was the fact that our two wins were in consecutive years. Part of the reason why we accomplished this difficult task was that we had a clear and goal-oriented mission statement. All of the ownership, executives, coaching staff, doctors, ball boys, equipment managers, and of course the 53 on our roster understood not just what the obvious goal was, but also how we envisioned reaching it.

The Greatest Mission Statement Ever

You should have strong clarity surrounding not only just the importance of a mission statement, but also how you can begin to create and implement such a statement for your business. However, to hammer the point home, let's consider one of the greatest mission statements ever given.

Take a look at this selection from President John F. Kennedy's speech discussing putting a man on the moon in his special message to Congress on urgent national needs on May 25, 1961:

> First, I believe that this nation should commit itself to achieving the goal, before this decade is out, of landing a man on the Moon and returning him safely to the Earth. . . . But in a very real sense, it will not be one man going to the Moon—if we make this judgment affirmatively, it will be an entire nation. For all of us must work to put him there. . . .
>
> This decision demands a major national commitment of scientific and technical manpower, materiel and

facilities, and the possibility of their diversion from other important activities where they are already thinly spread. It means a degree of dedication, organization and discipline which have not always characterized our research and development efforts. It means we cannot afford undue work stoppages, inflated costs of material or talent, wasteful interagency rivalries, or a high turnover of key personnel. . . .

Every scientist, every engineer, every serviceman, every technician, contractor, and civil servant [must give] his personal pledge that this nation will move forward, with the full speed of freedom, in the exciting adventure of space.

Think about this for a second. JFK's mission was to put a man on the moon, and through this clear and concise objective statement, he told an entire nation of individuals exactly how that would happen. If one man can inspire the dream of a nation and inevitably accomplish his mission, then we all have the ability, motivation, and know-how to formulate the perfect goal-driven statement to inspire our employees.

Teams at Work 4: The Greatest Team Ever

There is a great deal of talk about which was the greatest team ever. Was it the 1985 Chicago Bears? The Bulls in the 1990s? Maybe even the Patriots in the twenty-first century? Well, the greatest "dream team" we have ever seen may be the team that constructed *Apollo 11*. The Apollo space program was the follow-on to Project Mercury, and it became a focal point for NASA after President John F. Kennedy's challenge "of landing a man on the Moon and returning him safely to the Earth." *Apollo 11* became the realization of this national goal. The final financial cost to the American people was reported as $25.4 billion in 1973, and some 400,000 men and women diligently worked as engineers, flight directors, camera designers, software experts, suit testers, telescope crew members, aerospace technicians, photo developers, seamstresses, and navigators. Think about it—it took 400,000 people to put just a few men on the moon. And it was worth it.

Making Neil Armstrong and Buzz Aldrin, along with Michael Collins in the command module, the first men on the moon was an arduous and difficult task requiring dedication and determination. But it was one that was worth every ounce of blood, sweat, and tears. "Each crewman of *Apollo 11* had made a spaceflight before this mission, making it only the second all-veteran crew (the other being *Apollo 10*) in human spaceflight history." On July 21, 1969, an American man took the first steps on the moon. By modern-day standards, this accomplishment may seem like another day at the office, but over the course of a 200-hour journey to and from the moon, we made history. In fact, this may be considered the greatest task ever accomplished by a team. No sports team has anything on what this dedicated and determined team of 400,000 men and women succeeded in doing. ("Apollo 11," *Wikipedia*, January 11, 2013.)

FUDES for Thought

By now your mission should be stated. It should be apparent and at the forefront of your initiatives. But conceiving this statement is just the first step in the process. Next, you have to figure out how to integrate the mission into the inner workings of your business. It should fold into the fabric and become an interwoven piece of the material. It will become the glue that binds the energy of the team and directs it toward the efficient use of resources in completing the mission.

Let's revisit the example of building a house. You can hire a crew of 12 men who are skilled in masonry, carpentry, architecture, plumbing, electrical work, and many other areas. Then you can buy stacks of lumber, piles of bricks, sacks of nails, lengths of pipe, rolls of electric cord, bags of concrete, and all the other materials the workers may need. You can acquire the land, have the necessary permits in hand, have perfect timing with the weather, and so on and so forth. But until you set in motion the purpose for bringing all this together, it just sits there on the lot. The weather changes for the worse, the resources begin to deteriorate, the workers become tired and agitated, the county pulls the permits, and no house is built.

Thus, you have to create a catalyst for building your house, or all will be for naught. The same is true with your business and its mission statement. If you do not surround a strong objective with a vehicle and a method to apply and execute the plan, it will simply fall flat. So, you have to consider the catalyst for your company's mission statement. This is the jet pack that rockets it to the moon. And that is where FUDES for thought comes into play.

FUDES is an acronym standing for Focus + Unity + Direction + Excellence = Success. It is essentially a modern-day equation defining how to bring your mission statement to life.

FUDES really acts as the catalyst for bringing all your resources together. It takes the mission, whether it is to construct a house, to build a football team, or to make money, and sets in motion the personnel, hammers, nails, lumber, and everything else needed to accomplish the mission.

FUDES is the "mad scientist" of developing and implementing your mission statement, taking all the ingredients and mixing and matching them to build your company. If you strike the perfect balance among the elements of FUDES, the result will be a harmonious experience. However, if you mess up one of the elements, you will fall short of your objectives, and it will sound like an elementary school chorus—off key.

As the road map for your mission statement, FUDES guides it and helps you navigate the journey to eventual success. This concept is the result of looking at every facet of an organization: every situation and scenario it faces, every bit of energy or resources that is expended, every decision that is made—everything. All of it relates back to one of these five crucial factors as they pertain to achieving the mission.

For instance, over the course of my NFL career and building and running a team, all of the day-to-day responsibilities and behaviors were anchored in a combination of the mission statement and the FUDES acronym. Whether it was using the media to keep the team unified and focused, developing detailed plans and procedures to give direction to the players and streamline their efforts, setting standards of excellence and keeping everyone unified and on the same page, or even hiring and firing to maintain focus by stressing excellence, these four pieces would eventually funnel down to the inevitable success of the team. Essentially, the team would come to understand and truly believe that Focus + Unity + Direction + Excellence = Success.

At this point, let's break down FUDES even further so that you can see how each element should interact and play a role with your mission statement and ultimately your organization.

Focus

Though we're going to speak about broad mission statements, the end must be something tangible that the group can see all its efforts and resources constantly moving toward. It's very difficult to focus on smoke, or anything else that is dense but that dissipates. It's much easier to focus on concrete objectives and those ideas that are anchored to a belief system. I always tell companies that their employees should be focused on something that is not easily attained, but is clearly attainable. You have to set your sights on climbing the mountain, not climbing to the clouds.

This is done through continually focusing, unifying, directing, and demanding excellence toward the "light." This does not become redundant if it is integrated in the proper manner, and if you consistently ask, "What are we here for?" Done properly, this is like wearing a yellow Livestrong bracelet. You don't notice it there every waking second of the day, but it is there. You're reminded to Livestrong in order to stay focused and overcome adversity.

Consider the Livestrong manifesto:

We believe in life.
Your life.
We believe in living every minute of it with every ounce of
  your being.
And that you must not let cancer take control of it.
We believe in energy: channeled and fierce.
We believe in focus: getting smart and living strong.
Unity is strength. Knowledge is power. Attitude is everything.
This is LIVESTRONG.

For those who are wearing the bracelet, it takes only a passing glance, a quick visual reminder of the mission of Livestrong. Livestrong offers an example of how focusing on one single goal, beating cancer, can become a mantra, a slogan, and an inspiration to all. The same is true in business. Focus is the first step in the process of transforming your mission statement into a reality.

Just like that of Livestrong, your company's objective should be clear enough that any employee or new hire can understand exactly what it is, but involved enough so that it offers guidance and advice on how to attain it. Tony Robbins said, "One reason so few of us achieve what we truly want is that we never direct our focus; we never concentrate our power. Most people dabble their way through life, never deciding to master anything in particular." Focusing our efforts and energy on one goal or objective is something that each of us rarely does. As a leader, it is your responsibility to find ways to streamline the exertion of your workforce toward just that — one thing. Once you accomplish this task, you will channel the full potential that your team members can offer.

Unity

The second step to the FUDES process is enhancing your work environment by bringing your team members together and unifying them. Alexandre Dumas famously wrote in *The Three Musketeers*, "All for one and one for all." As much of a cliché as this may be, our undivided goal is to get everyone to buy in, go all in, and stay in. Your employees may be individual parts of the same thing, but they should always feel like and be viewed by outsiders as one entity.

Your mission should be something that all team members are willing to buy into. Ownership is critically important. It may come through shared beliefs, parallel visions, or some other mechanism. There may be differing opinions on how to get there, but ultimately everyone should want to get there together. With the true spirit of unification, all members should be willing to give their maximum effort and performance levels to achieve the ultimate end, while simultaneously realizing that they can't do so unless everyone does the same.

Unity can be developed through core cultural principles, but team building today requires even more of an effort to convince team members of the benefits to the individuals of accomplishing the mission, and that these benefits can't and won't ever be realized without the combined unified effort that builds strength through the multiplication of both personnel and resources.

Jeff Pash is the executive vice president and general counsel for the NFL. *Bloomberg Businessweek* has called him one of 100 most influential people in sports today. When speaking with him about team development and the value of unity within the overall team concept, he said:

> *To build team unity, you should recognize nobody's in a position to have all the answers or make all the decisions. So as a leader, you must trust others, hire good people, and build a strong team. Let them do their job, don't stand over their shoulders and micromanage them, second-guess them, or be afraid to allow them to make a decision.*
>
> *Be available; be supportive; have an open door for people who want to bounce ideas off of you. Show confidence in those that want to be part of your team, recognize and celebrate their strengths, and don't be scared that they may know more about something than you do.*

Unity will frequently be achieved through shared trials, tribulations, and failures. It requires the ability to persevere through these issues and ultimately come out stronger as a result of combined and unified efforts. The best teams are unified through intense pressure that forces their members to rely on one another in a myriad of ways. Whatever the case may be, no one can argue with the idea that together more can be achieved. By instilling a culture that supports a feeling of harmony, your company will be better positioned to reach all of its goals.

Direction

Now that your team is focused and unified, it is imperative that you offer it direction. This direction starts with the mission statement, but that is not enough. You must lead your team in the direction in which you desire it to go. This can be done in many ways, but detailed plans and procedures that give direction to and understanding of effort is always a smart place to start.

Leaders have the responsibility for drawing up the "plays" and offering direction as to how to execute them. There may be countless countermeasures and plan Bs, but ultimately the team members must take the knowledge of what the team is trying to accomplish, expend mental and physical energies toward executing the details, and then react to the dynamics of the situation itself. Business owners are rarely looking for robots on the field, but they do want employees who can understand the big picture, recognize changes that are taking place, and react accordingly to set things back in the direction of the big picture.

Often, this can require significant training in order to internalize and provide for the ability to act "outside the box" if and when required. The more you can visualize the main route, the easier it is to navigate detours and then eventually get back on track. However, part of providing direction to your employees is telling them where to go while also providing enough wiggle room so that they can figure out how to get there. If you trust your employees, this shouldn't be an issue or a problem.

Diving even deeper, direction requires giving constructive and critical feedback in a timely manner. Just as in all businesses, in the NFL, most players will tell you that the number one weakness of most clubs is their inability to communicate with and provide feedback to the players effectively. The players just don't know where they stand with the organization. Not only is this ineffective leadership, but it also is a waste of resources. If a team member is not performing up to standards, explaining how she can improve prevents waste and generally enhances performance.

Let individuals know where and how they fit into the overall efforts of the organization. We have so many ways to communicate with one another in today's world, and yet we may be experiencing the worst levels of personal and team communication ever seen. To offer direction to employees, this has to change for the better, and there should be a constant focus on talking, listening, and implementing what you hear into directives.

So direction for a team should act as the foundation and structural elements and should be used as the framework for executing with excellence.

Excellence

The final input in the equation for FUDES comes in the form of excellence. Once your team is focused and unified and has been given direction, it should work toward creating an environment of excellence. The notion of excellence can be difficult to define. Who determines the level of excellence required, strived for, and attained? How is it measured, and what is it measured against? This can be different for each and every company.

Excellence in today's society and across different generational and cultural gaps is often in the eye of the beholder.

One leader's "good enough" is another leader's "subpar." But excellence is also something that must be built into the culture of the organization. It must be something that the team itself can recognize and strive for without having a scorecard. Today, the prevailing attitude is that "good enough" is not necessarily good enough. Most important, anything and everything that is done toward the accomplishment of the mission should be done with the highest level of execution. If you can instill this attitude within your company, you are on your way to achieving excellence.

The top teams in any industry understand this idea. They put forth a little more effort, spend a little more time, and always do more than is necessary. This starts way back with selecting the right types of people, those who understand that the difference between 100 percent and 110 percent isn't just 10 percent. When these individuals are focused on a mission that they believe in, and when they have been given the proper tools and direction, they will inherently unify with others. Then, and only then, can what was once good enough truly become great. The best companies and winning sports teams covet these types of team members.

It All Equals Success

The inevitable product of F, U, D, and E can be nothing but success. There is no other direction in which to proceed. It is like a train heading full speed down the tracks, leaving everything behind it. When energy and resources are multiplied by a cohesive and focused unity of effort to reach an ultimate goal, these efforts will move so fluidly and with such precision that no conflicting outside force will be strong enough to offset their purposeful motion. The team will reach its destination. The product of focus, unity, direction, and excellence is success. Just as fire creates smoke, wind forms waves, and clouds create rain, when you implement this powerful formula as the catalyst for your mission statement, success will follow 100 percent of the time.

True satisfaction based on success is chased by many and reached by few. However, it can be achieved through the final accomplishment of the mission, and by reaching benchmarks and other subgoals as well. Dale Carnegie said, "The person who gets the farthest is generally the one who is willing to do and dare. The sure-thing boat never gets far from shore." The FUDES equation is not easy. It takes hard work and dedication to your cause. However, if you dare to try it and meticulously labor to implement it, there is no doubt that you will go as far as you desire.

Teams at Work 5: The London Games

In August of 2012, more than 10,000 athletes from over 204 National Olympic Committees participated in London's third hosting of the Olympics. They competed in dozens of sports and represented their respective nations with inspiring pride. Each athlete entered these games with a team behind him. This team may have been made up of only a few loved ones, or it may have included a whole host of trainers and experts.

But with each athlete comes a story of teamwork and individuals working together to succeed.

At the beginning of the journey, London was just one of numerous cities that were bidding to call the Olympics their own. They journey began in the summer of 2003, when bids were submitted by nine international cities. London had to withstand two years of selection review before it was awarded the games. The organizing committee met three months later to begin overseeing the staging of the games, which was coordinated by the Government Olympic Executive.

A mixture of new, existing, and historic venues, along with some temporary facilities, were used for the events. The costs of the games were mostly privately funded through the International Olympic Committee, but the construction of facilities and other infrastructure, along with redevelopment of the Olympic Park area, was financed through public funding. Millions of dollars were spent on strategies to maximize the impact of the 2012 Olympic Games. London was the center of the world for a summer.

Unpaid volunteers were a vital source of personnel to help with a variety of tasks both before and during the London Olympics. In 2004, the organizers had estimated a need for some 70,000 volunteers, but they received more than 240,000 applications in 2010. More than 8 million volunteer hours were put into hosting the games.

Security operations were enforced by 10,000 police officers, supported by another 13,500 members of the armed forces. Both air and naval assets were utilized, with ships, jets, and surface-to-air missiles being employed. It was one of the biggest British security operations in decades. The Olympic Torch Relay ran from May 19 to July 27, 2012, with more than 8,000 participants carrying the torch for more than 70 days and some 8,000 miles. Great Britain achieved its highest total of gold medals since 1908 and finished third overall on the podium. From the athletes training for the games, to the committee from London that was meticulously working to call the Olympics a part of history, to the thousands of volunteers working to represent the United Kingdom, to the teams of players going for the gold, the common thread tying everyone together was teamwork. (Based on "2012 Summer Olympics," *Wikipedia*, January 28, 2013.)

Turning Cogs into a Unified Team

By spending time focusing your employees, unifying them in a particular direction, and demanding excellence wherever you may lead, you will begin to reach new heights of success. But to fully reach your goals, it is crucial that you instill a feeling of belief in the ultimate message. People have to buy into your vision and mission. This begins from within through ensuring that members are truly part of the FUDES process. By nature, employees want to support your mission. But to create an environment where they believe in your vision, you have to do more.

As a child, I had a toy that was made up of a set of about two dozen plastic cogs. There were big cogs, little cogs, green cogs, and red cogs. Individually, each of them was nothing more than a wheel with teeth around its outer circumference. The objective of the toy was to arrange the cogs in such a way that when you were finished, you could turn a handle and each and every cog would turn in conjunction with the others. When the cogs were properly assembled, there was precise movement throughout—synergy at its finest. But all it took was misplacing one piece of this "cog puzzle" for the toy to no longer work. In business, when team members understand that they are integral pieces of the overall puzzle and know that the machine cannot move without their help, great things can happen. They will believe in both you as a leader and your business as a potential success.

The toy allowed you to see this idea at work, but the greater challenge is getting team members to understand it. To do this, team leaders have to allow team members to see the inner workings of the organization or the company, and to see how a lack of focus, poor unity, misguided direction, and low standards of excellence will never lead to eventual success. That is how you make your employees believers. Show them how it works, and stress the point that without their cooperation and dedication to the mission, success will be unattainable.

The workers in this generation are looking to see how they fit into the process. They do not want to just be purple cogs. They have to see that when one cog is removed, the team shuts down—that a maximized individual, in every facet of her role in the team, makes for a stronger force multiplier.

The Mission to Create a Family Environment

The mission statement should be clearly mirrored in the culture and environment of the company. Earlier, we spoke of the value of your mission being found in the fabric of your culture. However, to take this one step further, consider the best setting for the development and growth of a mission statement and the FUDES process.

In nature, the core teams are families: the male and female of the species working to protect their offspring and willing to do whatever is necessary to achieve this. The same holds true for most of us. Our first lessons in teamwork (good or bad) come through the family dynamic. The strongest teams are those whose members act as if they were one family, relying on one another for support and for necessities. Families set goals, disagree, face challenges, expand, grow, die, and divert. There are matriarchs, patriarchs, gifted members, and those with special needs. Yet by and large, regardless of the culture, at least in the family setting, the individual remains intensely loyal to the family unit.

Family members are willing to fight through all the bad and share in all the good. They must communicate with and respect one another in order to maintain strength. There are understood roles and responsibilities of the father, the mother, the eldest son or daughter, and younger siblings. Wisdom is passed down from the more experienced members, often grandparents or aunts and uncles.

A family environment develops this communication process, fosters respect for one another regardless of the circumstances, calls for members to wear the "team name" with pride and represent it well, and encourages team members to look to their more experienced colleagues for wisdom and historical perspective regarding the efforts of the team.

When you view your team as an extension of your family and form an environment and a mission statement that reflects this viewpoint, you will find that your team will not only appreciate this, but also work harder for you and your business. You can do this by spending time with employees; getting to know them, their backgrounds, and their concerns and aspirations; and understanding all of their weaknesses and strengths—just as you do with your own family.

Dana Perino served as White House press secretary for President George W. Bush and is a nationally renowned media strategist and an active participant in the national political debate. She is president of Dana Perino and Co., a company that provides public affairs, messaging, and media strategies to clients from a wide range of industry sectors. She told me:

> *There is no possible way to be an effective press secretary without a loyal, energized, and knowledgeable team. I had a rule in my office that if I ever was surprised by a question in the briefing room, then somebody hadn't done their job. And I think that happened only once, and it wasn't someone's fault—it was a nutty question from a reporter who didn't frequent the briefings. I always made sure my team felt included in the good parts of the job—at the White House, that often means access to the president. I would let them fill in for me in policy meetings or at the podium, showing that I trusted them and that we were stronger together when we were knitted up for a common purpose.*

*Every day since I left the White House, I communicate
with someone from my team from those days. We were more
than friends; we were family, and I would do it all again if
I could assemble that same group.*

Dana's attitude demonstrates the value for leaders in general
of viewing their team as a family.

You must set high standards for conduct, morals, character, integrity, and communication, and then be the absolute
best at living up to those standards. You must serve as the example for all. There is this search for building good teams in the
workplace, and yet there are outstanding examples of both good
and bad all around. However, when you are creating a mission
statement and working to integrate it into the very fabric of
your employees, you have to motivate and inspire them to buy
into the process. Through establishing surroundings that focus
on family and the close-knit relationships often associated with
those closest to you, you will find that your employees feel nurtured and welcome the opportunity and honor to fulfill your
mission statement and buy into the FUDES process.

Teams at Work 6: One World Trade Center

We all know it as one of the saddest days in American history.
Cowards victimized us, and the manner in which we live our
lives was changed in an instant.

Following the destruction of the original World Trade
Center on September 11, 2001, there was much debate
regarding [what to do with the land on which the World

Trade Center had once stood. In] 2003 the Lower Manhattan Development Corporation organized a competition to determine how to use the site.

The current "Freedom Tower" design by architect Daniel Libeskind won the competition to replace the two towers and was unveiled in June of 2005.

Numerous issues ranging from security to aesthetics to emotions have influenced changes in the overall plans and developmental design. Architect David Childs took over the day-to-day operations and

> is responsible for overseeing its . . . design development from inception to completion. . . . Dan Tishman and his father, John Tishman, builder of the original World Trade Center, [were the primary construction management team of 1 WTC.] Douglas and Jody Durst, co-presidents of the Durst Organization, . . . won the right to invest at least $100 million in the project. The Durst organization . . . specializes in the development, managing, leasing, and operation of sustainable commercial construction space. . . .
>
> Nearly all of the construction workers interviewed praised the unity and work ethic of the new World Trade Center's construction team. Others spoke of the importance they believed the construction of the tower had to the people of the United States. A deputy foreman . . . said, "All the men are working in conjunction to put this building up. They all know how important this is to the country—and to show the world what us Americans can do—and get this done, union and proud." Another

deputy foreman . . . commented, "[The] camaraderie of the crew is very good." . . .

The tower's construction was partly funded with approximately $1 billion of insurance money recouped . . . in connection with the September 11 attacks. The State of New York provided $250 million toward construction costs, and the Port Authority agreed to finance a further $1 billion through the sale of bonds. . . .

At the time of its completion in 2013, One World Trade Center will be the tallest building in the Western Hemisphere and the third-tallest building in the world by pinnacle height, with its spire reaching a symbolic 1,776 feet . . . in reference to the year of American independence.

It was just a few cowards that brought the original World Trade Center down, but it was a united team of millions of Americans that offered the inspiration, the motivation, and the effort to rebuild it bigger and better. When all is said and done, 1 WTC will be more than 100 stories tall. But it will also stand as a beacon for what we can accomplish, how we can bounce back, and the steadfast notion that we are all part of the same team. (From "One World Trade Center," *Wikipedia*, January 29, 2013.)

The Payoff of Your Mission

When you have built a strong mission statement through the FUDES method, you will find that you are capable of filtering and funneling each and every effort and aspect of your operations. Team members will always know what everyone is working toward. No man or woman will be too big, no task too small—everyone will be on the same page. New members will immediately understand the purpose of the team and the organization they are joining, as well as how their skills might be utilized. Through this process, you will also explain why energy and resources are directed in a particular manner so that team members can decide whether this is something worthwhile and something that is worthy of their efforts and affiliation.

Motivation and self-worth as they relate to personal effort and production can be measured by each individual's understanding and realization of his contribution to the overall efforts of the team toward the goal, as directives and how eventual *success* can be reached are spelled out clearly to all. High standards and expectations of excellence bring forth the best efforts of the team members involved, and if only the best and the brightest who perform at the highest levels are retained by your team while the subpar performers and underachievers are weeded out, the team will be strong and will survive.

But it all comes down to your mission statement. It is the "light" that forces an economy of effort and the efficient use of resources by those involved with the team.

CHAPTER 3

THE DEVELOPMENT: MAXIMIZING PERFORMANCE

n the first two chapters of this book, we spent time discussing how you can identify the best employees available from a large and growing pool. We then focused on creating a specific mission statement and implementing it within your organization so that you can maintain your focus and drive your new hires forward in a meaningful and efficient manner. With those lessons in hand, we now turn to developing new hires and current talent and maximizing their performance.

The first step in understanding this concept is shifting your thought process from the old ideas of team development, which don't necessarily work anymore. Some of today's team members might fall in line, but to maximize their performance and that of the overall team, it is crucial that you modify your perspective to one that is centered on a strong developmental approach.

Many team leaders do not know how to do this and do not see the necessity for doing so. It takes an enormous amount of effort and meticulous attention to detail. Senior managers can get lost in their focus on the mission, as that is normally what they are paid to accomplish. These managers lack the appreciation, awareness, and belief that it takes every cog in the machine to achieve your company's goals, and that those cogs are less likely to react positively and let you lead them simply because you said this is what they should do.

Far too often, we position ourselves to accept the ways of the past and forget the value of change. Whether it is in the NFL or in business, the talent pool that organizations are growing from is made up of a new and younger generation.

Being a professional athlete doesn't make someone immune to his own generation's culturally developed norms in dealing with workplace and societal issues. Thus, general managers, coaches, and executives are constantly struggling to find ways in which they can develop and maximize talent at this high level. Often management just adopts the archaic way of thinking and continues with the accepted ways of handling the previous generation. It is time to take these obsolete and inefficient developmental processes and change them. Given that limited resources and are finances available, hiring at value and then developing talent and maximizing performance are at a premium.

Bruce Tulgan is internationally recognized as the leading expert on young people in the workplace and one of the leading experts on leadership and management. Bruce is a bestselling author, an advisor to business leaders all over the world, and a sought-after keynote speaker and management trainer. In our interview, he said, "The enemy of change is habit. People are in their comfort zones, especially in their day-to-day working relationships. They get in their comfort zones, and it's a little uncomfortable to hold people to a higher standard and insist they reach it." As we move through this chapter, we will discuss some of the most powerful and effective ways you can change the lens through which you view the development process and capitalize on the talent you spent endless resources on hiring and training. Change is difficult, but the results of this investment are sky-high.

Developing the Extraordinary

No one in this world wants to be ordinary. On every level, average is simply not good enough. It is not accepted, welcomed, or celebrated. But when it comes to developing and training employees, we do so in a way that promotes the notion of the ordinary. It is time to change that practice. The value of the extraordinary is immeasurable. Orison Swett Marden said, "Don't wait for extraordinary opportunities. Seize common occasions and make them great. Weak men wait for opportunities; strong men make them." Today, leaders and employees alike squander the occasions to do great things, go big, and create extraordinary results. It starts with the training and development of new employees and trickles down to the type of environment and workplace you create. In the end, your attitude will inspire or suppress the appetite of your team.

The extraordinary is the idea of building upon predicted potential. Every team starts with a finite number of individuals with various backgrounds and training. Through detailed development and provided opportunity, you can train your team members to not just meet standards, but also exceed them. We already discussed the importance of finding the best and the brightest and setting a mission statement with well-conceived plans and procedures. But now it is time to maximize the production and output of each member at the individual level, the subgroup level, and the entirety of the team.

The team and its leadership should encourage its members to strive for excellence through continuing education and development opportunities. If and when possible, a team member should look and/or ask for these very opportunities. The strongest teams will foster this through programs built to strengthen the individual cogs in the machine. Team and corporate resources are commonly more abundant than those of the individual. By choosing the best and the brightest, then taking their talent to the next level through opportunity, training, and experience, you can quickly create extraordinary team members.

In our interview, Bruce Tulgan indicated, "The competitive landscape is pretty evened out on recruiting, but there is a huge room for competitive advantage for the team focusing on intensive development and cultivation. That team is going to optimize the talent. If everyone is bringing in the same level of talent, but one team decides to pour resources into the development process, it is going to optimize its talent at a much higher level." The team or organization that has a well-thought-out, detailed, and efficiently implemented plan for training and developing its members will almost always come out on top when talent is equal. Being extraordinary starts with you—the leader. Extraordinary attention to training and development will lead directly to extraordinary performance and results.

But this has to be a way of life and a method of thought, not just a warm and heartfelt concept. You have to change your thinking to reflect a focus on maximizing talent to achieve extraordinary results, while rejecting the archaic and outdated approach of "hire and fire." Employees are assets, and assets should be nurtured, cultivated, and positioned to excel.

Teams at Work 7: *The Lord of the Rings*—"Hobbits and Middle-earth"
Director Peter Jackson's *The Lord of the Rings* movie trilogy was the film adaptation of J. R. R. Tolkien's famous three-volume book of the same name. The films (*The Fellowship of the Ring, The Two Towers*, and *The Return of the King*) were all done simultaneously and are considered one of the biggest and most ambitious movie projects ever. It took eight years to complete the entire project at a cost of $285 million, and it became the most successful film series of all time, grossing $2.92 billion at the box office and garnering 17 Academy Awards from 30 nominations. The three movies were filmed in more than 150 different locations by seven different units, and on soundstages in Wellington and Queenstown, New Zealand.

Jackson oversaw the entire production, but he utilized five other directors along with assistant directors, producers, and writers. He monitored the units via live satellite feeds. To minimize pressure, he hired different editors for each film (a total of five), who pored over some six million feet of film (more than 1,100 miles). Technicians worked throughout New Zealand to get many of the sounds, once using some 20,000 cricket fans to generate the sound of an attacking army.

The New Zealand army itself helped build "Hobbiton," and movie workshops built and assembled 48,000 pieces of armor, 500 bows, 10,000 arrows, and 1,800 pairs of hobbit feet, along with ears, noses, and heads, and some 40 seamstresses created 19,000 costumes for the cast. The cast was also extensively trained over six weeks in sword fighting, horseback riding, and boating techniques. The New Zealand Symphony, the London Philharmonic, and the London Voices all contributed to the musical score for the three films.

These movies represented what is widely considered one of the most riveting and amazing examples of teamwork in the movie industry. Watching any of the three movies will provide one of the most visually stunning and impactful movie experiences you will ever have. The number of moving parts that had to be optimized and interwoven by a team of professionals is unimaginable. However, the end result is simply mind-altering. (Based on "*The Lord of the Rings* (film series)," *Wikipedia*, January 29, 2013.)

Investments, Not Commodities

Today's generation of young team members is more than willing to contribute to team situations, but these people want to know that their efforts will be rewarded at the personal level as well. They immediately begin looking for an out if they feel that the team and its leaders are not there to support them. Thus, it is vital to team development to create an environment in which all members feel that they are appreciated and seen as investments rather than as movable and disposable commodities.

A commodity is something with a finite supply or a known quantity. It's used, burnt, or otherwise spent, and then it is no more. If today's team members feel as if they are nothing more than "fuel for the machine," they will seek opportunity elsewhere—not an efficient way to develop top talent for your team.

Without a clear direction or understood plan for the individual, team members may become complacent regarding their role in the accomplishment of the mission. In some instances, it takes only one downtrodden or disgruntled team member to destroy the efforts of the entire team and set back whatever progress has been made toward the final destination.

If you view your team members as commodities, it will become increasingly difficult for you to attract the best and the brightest. Today's communication conduits make the world a very small place. The workforce is constantly collaborating, and since most of us are looking for the same things from our affiliation with a team, lack of a clear direction for the individual can quickly spell doom for teams that are looking to add top talent.

Motivation toward excellence is always enhanced when team members feel that the organization truly cares about them and has created an infrastructure to support, foster, and enhance the team members' personal and professional growth. Team members begin to feel like valuable assets over time. They are then willing to put forth the extra effort to create extraordinary results. This shows up in how they interact with one another, how they interact with clients and customers, and how they interact with the leadership and upper management.

Creating an environment in which team members feel that they are an investment and an asset is imperative for your business. Everyone wants to be heard and appreciated at some level. Tom Osborne coached football at the University of Nebraska for 25 years. While he was there, he won more games and had a better winning percentage than any other coach during his tenure. After coaching, Osborne was elected to Congress in 2000 and served six years in the U.S. House of Representatives as a Republican from Nebraska's Third District. He then returned to Nebraska to become its current athletic director. He told me:

> *I think the players at Nebraska felt cared for. We tried to make sure they understood that whether they were on the first team or fourth team, we cared about them as people, cared about their education, cared about their health, cared about their families, and even knew all of their names. Where they were on the depth chart didn't make any difference in our concern and care for them. Over time, we developed a culture such that players realized that when the team won, everybody won. And as a result we sometimes had players make great sacrifices to play. Some would stay on the scout team for three years, even four years. We tried to emphasize that everyone had a role to play; whether he was a starter or a scout team player, he made a significant contribution. Each player was an invaluable asset.*

When you invest in your team, your team will invest in you. Great leaders understand this concept and push for it within their teams. They invest time, money, and resources and get the same in return from their employees. It is important that the individual not only is a solid team member in the traditional definition, but also puts heavy emphasis upon improving and maximizing her own skills to increase her value. Strong individuals make for a stronger team.

More than anything, though, team leaders must treat their team with respect and go the extra mile to ensure that no one feels disposable or unwanted. Everyone has a profound effect on the bottom line, and even one disgruntled employee is far too many.

Implementing Your New Culture

The concepts of promoting extraordinary work, viewing employees as assets, and motivating team members to create personal corporations are all part of implementing a culture of team success and unity. Imagine that a company is a garden and the team members within that company are fruits and vegetables. The end goal is to grow healthy produce or strong employees. Just as you water a garden and ensure that seeds are planted correctly and do not impinge upon one another, you train your team members and nurture their growth. However, to accelerate growth in any garden, a gardener will ensure that the soil is rich in nutrients and offers the seeds a setting that can maximize their growth and health. The same is true in business. A positive culture for an employee is like a nutrient-rich soil for a vegetable—it promotes development and progression.

Consider these valuable resources that can create a nutrient-rich culture for team members that promotes growth and maximizes development.

Mentorship

It's possible to accelerate the acceptance of a team's culture through horizontal and vertical mentorship. To draw upon nature once again, let's look at the wolf pack. A lot of the basic survival instincts are taught by the pup's parents. The pup imprints the behavior of the adults and leans on them for early survival. Basic lessons are taught through learned behavior and the dominant role of the parents. As the pups begin to mature, they lean more upon their siblings and upon wolves from other litters. Here, usually through play and early hunting experiences, the wolf pup assimilates into the role of a member of the pack.

To indoctrinate new personnel into an organization's culture effectively, team leaders would be well advised to ensure that the new members have a solid understanding of the organization's mission, the role the team members will play in accomplishing that mission, and a clear appreciation for the plans and procedures used to carry out these responsibilities.

Clearly the best way to create this is through internal mentorship that works both from the top down and within the team member's own line of responsibility. Strong teams have leaders who are willing to get involved in the development of new talent. They set standards and expectations, provide resources for understanding and improvement, and then give critical feedback and constructive guidance. It's easy to "talk the talk," but team leaders must also "walk the walk" and make themselves both open and available to enhance their assets.

Within every team, there are horizontal lines of responsibility. Veteran employees who perform the exact same function as new talent can pass along the accepted norms of the team both by example and by one-on-one interaction. New team members who are open to peer input can quickly learn how to assimilate into the team culture through the knowledge and experience of longtime members.

Here lies the importance of vertical mentorship at every level of the team, regardless of position or experience. The tendency is to allow the more senior members to begin to operate on their own as constructive feedback slowly wanes. Team leaders must continue to clarify the mission and the role of every member, even as the team changes through expansion and contraction, success or failure.

Feedback

To ensure that your culture is going in the right direction, you have to keep your ear to the street. It is crucial to understand how your employees view your organization's culture and what you can do to enhance it.

Tom Osborne discussed the most powerful method to enhance a culture and the employee or team attitude. He said,

> To build culture, we created a "Unity Council." We had the players select two players from each position on the team. We had 16 players on the Unity Council and charged

them with bringing up anything they saw occur that prevented team unity. They would meet every Tuesday night with the strength coach, and they were free to bring up anything they heard or saw. These concerns would then be relayed to me the following morning, and I would address them with the team. It was a lot of stuff that you normally wouldn't hear about.

Maybe they didn't like what they had for lunch the previous day, or the movie I selected before we played a certain team. Most of these things we addressed rather quickly. We'd make sure we changed the menu or let them pick the movie. As a result, a lot of things came to my attention that I would probably never have heard. I think the players also felt that this was a form of caring, a form of recognizing their worth, and a way to give them a voice. We allowed the players to set the goals for the season as well and adopted those goals as our own. Again, they were given that voice. Once we started this practice, it was amazing how many of those goals we accomplished. They were pretty lofty, but we made the point that these are your goals and we'll help you do it, but it's up to you to accomplish them. So we gave the players some ownership as well.

You cannot fix what you don't know about. By creating a soundboard for feedback, you will position yourself to maximize employee happiness and minimize needless frustration. Amplifying the happiness of your team members will result in an expansion of your team's overall success. Make sure you create an environment with the availability to hear your employees' concerns.

Looking Outside the Box

A final element to emphasize in building a strong culture is to consider all options and think outside of the box. Tom Osborne was arguably the first coach to institute a Unity Council, but many teams now have a similar program for their players. Do not be afraid to go against the grain and create new and unique programs. By looking outside the box, you create a scenario in which you are looking for change, but also welcoming the advice and guidance of others. Think about what experts on culture and team management could do for your work environment and your employees. By utilizing these unbiased, specialized, and focused experts, you can bring about a change for the better in the culture of your team, as outsiders can evaluate your workplace conditions without being clouded by internal dynamics. They can further emphasize the importance of the task at hand and ensure its completion without being tainted by other requirements or responsibilities. This also demonstrates to your team a commitment to seek out the best people and resources. Not every organization can have experts in every field, but it can make certain that it has access to these experts.

The world has become a very detailed and specialized place. Some management and leadership positions within a team have been divided once, twice, or three times. This has just become the nature of things in today's fast-paced and ever-changing workplace. Trying to take on every aspect of individualized and specialized training and development is next to impossible. Above all, if you do, team members won't be getting the kind of high-level, high-standards training that you want them to receive. Many teams lack the personnel and resources to provide this type of training internally. Often the understanding and judgment concerning the need for added emphasis on a particular area is clouded by internal bias. However, if egos can be set aside and a meticulous screening of the environment can be completed, positive change can ensue.

Why not think outside of the box and bring in outside consultants? If they have a firm understanding of how their expertise in their discipline fits into the big picture of accomplishing your team's mission, they can better tailor these programs to help guide the team members toward success, without unknowingly showing partiality or prejudice toward other team members and/or team efforts. This all results in making the group stronger through the combined strength of all involved.

Each of the options mentioned is a powerful and compelling way to enhance and create a nutrient-rich culture for the development and maximization of your workforce. It calls for time, attention to detail, and dedicating yourself as a leader to changing the way you once thought. However, the attention will coincide with an improvement in employee attitude and an increase in output.

Teams at Work 8: Panama Canal

Described by the American Society of Civil Engineers as one of the Seven Wonders of the Modern World, the Canal was begun in 1881 and finished in 1914. Cutting through the Isthmus of Panama for 47.9 miles, it connects the Atlantic (via the Caribbean) to the Pacific Ocean. French construction began in 1881 (then was abandoned in 1889) and was picked up by the United States in 1904. The U.S. Army Corps of Engineers would dedicate thousands of workers and millions of dollars toward its eventual completion. Nearly all the equipment used was manufactured by new, extensive machine-building technology developed and built in the United States. The canal consists of artificial lakes, several improved and artificial channels, and three sets of locks. An additional artificial lake, Alajuela Lake, acts as a reservoir for the canal. After two years of extensive sanitation and mosquito abatement work, the mosquito-spread diseases were nearly eliminated. Extensive work, also involving thousands and costing millions, was done on preparing the infrastructure needed by the workers and their equipment. After the upgrading of the Panama Railroad and other preliminary work were completed, the construction of an elevated canal with locks began in earnest. The United States spent almost $375,000,000, including $12,000,000 to build facilities used to guard the canal, to finish the project. More than 60 million pounds of dynamite was used to excavate and construct the canal. This was by far the largest American engineering project of that or any previous era. About 5,600 workers died during this period (1904–1914), bringing the total death toll for the construction of the canal to around 27,500.

Early planners of the canal wisely thought ahead, anticipating that the width of cargo ships would probably increase in the future. However, the widths of modern-day cargo ships generally now exceed that so-called Panamax benchmark;

thus there are strict limits on which ships can fit through the locks. An expansion to double the waterway's capacity is set to be completed in 2014. Even more interesting is the fact that the Panama Canal transports 4 percent of world trade and 16 percent of total U.S.-borne trade. About 12,000 to 15,000 ships cross through the Panama Canal each and every year carrying hundreds of thousands of passengers. We often talk about teamwork at its finest, and the Panama Canal is by far one of the most impressive performances by a hardworking and well-organized group of people. (Based on "Panama Canal," *Wikipedia*, January 24, 2013.)

Personalized Development Plans (PDPs)

In addition to focusing on the culture of your workforce, you must realize that team members maintain an almost unquenchable desire to feel appreciated and attended to. It is your job to fulfill that desire and demonstrate appreciation and attention. This can become a bit of an arduous task, but in the end, you'll have stronger team members who are more understanding of and committed to the mission of the team and their role in it. It takes much more focus on the part of the team leadership to ensure that individualized plans for each member are designed and executed.

With that said, one of the most effective and efficient ways in which to build team momentum and maximize output is to create personalized development plans for team members. Once each of your team members views himself as a small but intertwined corporation, it is vital for all of them to feel that upper management and leadership has a well-thought-out and strategic business plan to maximize their success. That is where PDPs come into play.

Personalized plans solve three problems that most organizations find in employee training and development:

1. They allow leaders to evaluate employees and get to know them on a personal level.

2. They allow leaders to identify and emphasize the strengths of employees and capitalize on them.

3. Finally, they allow leaders to recognize areas of concern and positively increase performance.

PDPs allow you to not only get to know your employees at a very personal level, but also use their strengths while effectively eliminating their weaknesses. Team leaders would be well served by finding the strengths of each team member and expanding upon those areas in the overall development plan. Give the team member numerous opportunities to utilize the skills that bring out the full potential of her place within the group. Simultaneously, leaders can then attack the team member's weak areas by directly focusing on the skills and behavior needed to overcome those weaknesses. The team member must be fully aware of what the deficiency is, fully understand what must be done to improve upon it, and be given consistent and positive critiques.

PDPs are a checks-and-balances system with regard to the relationship between management and team members. If employees comprehend your desire and need to utilize them to their fullest potential, you'll create the kind of loyalty in your team members that very few companies, organizations, clubs, and teams ever realize.

There are numerous ways to implement a PDP program, but it generally requires the following viable elements:

o An understanding of the basic and advanced requirements for the position.

o Evaluating the capabilities and experience of each team member.

o Assessing employees' current status and ability.

o Working to enhance existing strengths and improve upon areas of weakness.

o Offering both training and real-world experience for the team member to practice and execute.

o Providing realistic timelines for the completion of training.

o Giving feedback and critical opinion of results.

In a team atmosphere, it's important that you develop an understanding and knowledge of your team members across the board. Ignoring this aspect of the team member–to–team leader relationship can often lead to misunderstandings, misinterpretations, and mismanagement, all of which affect the ultimate results and bottom line of your business.

Once you implement this program, never back off from the proposed plan between the team member and his trainers. Stick to the plan, consistently review it, and provide continuous feedback and monitoring of the team member's overall progress. Make sure that the developmental plan has real-world implications in terms of the team member's role and responsibilities.

Today's workers expect a lot from their employer and from other team members. By developing a well-thought-out developmental plan, you'll be providing an avenue for success for each member. What you need in exchange is her commitment to do her very best to stick with the plan and execute it on a daily, weekly, monthly, and yearly basis. PDPs are nothing more than a contract between you as a leader and your team members. The employee agrees to work hard, believe in the mission, and be a proactive piece of the puzzle. In return, you offer team members constant feedback and invest both time and resources into training and developing their skills and ability. When all is said and done, you will have a well-trained and strong employee, and the team member will have developed essential skills and tools to find success in his industry.

John Semcken, a former Navy fighter pilot, is currently vice president of Majestic Realty Co. When he joined the firm in 1996, he had primary responsibility for identifying, analyzing, and negotiating a site for a sports and entertainment complex to house Los Angeles's professional sports teams. This became the newly opened Staples Center. He told me in our interview,

> When it comes to maximizing team development, don't give them everything to run the race and then not let them out of the gate. Bring people onto the team for their expertise, and then focus time and effort on training them. You should hire people who find ways to make things happen, and who welcome feedback and training. As a Navy fighter

pilot, you depend on the guys on the ground to get you up in the air. It might be a cold, gloomy day and you're up there in the blue skies, having the fun flying in and over the cloud cover. Back down underneath, it's still cold and gloomy. But it was a specific group of people who gave you the tools you need to fly. Pay attention to the people and things that don't directly benefit you, as their work ultimately makes it happen.

John brings up a valuable point relating to the interconnectivity of the team members. We all play a role in the end result and the success of the business, so it is vital for all of us to invest and trust in one another. A PDP raises morale and demonstrates to employees just how much you care. It shows them that while you may be flying in the blue sky above the clouds day in and day out, you care about how they feel and what they need from the organization.

A personalized development plan program should be tailored toward your business and its ultimate goals. Regardless, the core principles consist of evaluating the employee and offering consistent feedback, investing in training of that employee, and focusing on capitalizing on the employee's strengths while eliminating her weaknesses.

Closing the Gap Between Management and Employees

At this point in the chapter, you should have a clear understanding of the process of developing and investing in employees to create extraordinary results, as well as of tools to maximize performance, such as building a nutrient-rich culture and implementing a personalized development plan. With all of those in mind, the final step in growing and maximizing team success is through closing the gap between management and employees. All the advice and guidance in this chapter has assumed an underlying desire to bridge the gap between upper management and employees. But like anything else that makes a difference, it has to be a conscious and determined effort if it is to really matter.

With that in mind, consider implementing the following valuable resources and programs to ensure that employees at all levels find comfort and commonality with those who manage and lead them.

Regular Reviews

We discussed this briefly earlier, but employees need structured and directed reviews. These offer an opportunity for two-way communication between leaders and team members. They raise morale and motivate employees to work hard, knowing that there is a definite and finite time when they will receive constructive feedback. Furthermore, these reviews should provide an occasion for raises, incentives, and bonuses. Offering an employee the knowledge that he will be in front of a superior and have a chance to be rewarded for quality performance and success can inspire hard work on a daily basis. Furthermore, this gives employees a chance to know where they stand and to work on issues that are of concern. If they do not know that they are doing something wrong, they will not be able to fix it.

Meet Them Halfway

Another way to bridge the gap between management and employees is to meet them in the middle. Far too often, employees feel that they are putting forth all the effort in the relationship. Your goal should be to find a common ground and both gravitate toward it. You each have responsibilities within the relationship between the employees and their boss, so it is imperative that you both hold up your end of the bargain. Your team members should work diligently to manifest your mission and serve your company in a positive manner. You should compensate and support your employees in a nutrient-rich environment that fosters growth and development. By meeting them in the middle, you demonstrate both your care and your concern for their needs, which will help to close the gap.

Open-Door Policy

It is not just about having an open-door policy; it is really about stressing it. Team members should always feel that they are welcome to walk into an upper manager's office with questions or concerns regarding the business or their position. This promotes positive communication and ensures that team members have a direct path to upper management. Again and again, companies indicate that they have an open-door policy, but the layout of the office and the closed doors indicate otherwise. Take the doors off their hinges if that's what it takes to keep them always open. Put a sign up on your door indicating that employees are always welcome to come in. If you do not take active steps to show your employees that your door is always open, they may never feel that it actually is.

Personalized Communication

We will discuss this in more depth later, but personalized communication from upper management to employees is vital to create a relationship between the two parties. Dr. Harvey Schiller is CEO of Global Options Group, a multidisciplinary international risk management and business solutions company. Prior to this position, Dr. Schiller was CEO of YankeeNets. His previous experience includes president of Turner Sports, Inc., executive director and secretary general of the U.S. Olympic Committee, and commissioner of the Southeastern Conference. Prior to joining the SEC, Dr. Schiller served for more than 25 years in the U.S. Air Force, achieving the rank of brigadier general.

He told me,

> *When I took over the U.S. Olympic Committee, I started out by writing a birthday card to everyone who ever won a gold medal and a birthday card to every International Olympic Committee member. Now I've expanded it to clients and so forth, signing a couple of hundred birthday cards every month. In fact, I will send ties or books to some people I'm closer to or have a closer relationship with. When you send them this handwritten correspondence, you'd be surprised how special it makes them feel. It really is all about those little things we talked about on how to keep that team together, I think that's part of it.*

Dr. Schiller further said, "I remember when former Major League Baseball manager Tommy Lasorda came to speak at the Air Force Academy and was asked the importance of getting to know his players. Lasorda then recited his entire starting lineup, along with each player's wife's name, children's name(s), and even their age(s). I went back to my department the next day and told my assistant to pull the names of all my employees and their families." The point is that this personalized communication and attention demonstrates to people that you care, you're dedicated to them, and you're available. There are far too many organizations where the disconnect between the leadership and the team members not only is evident, but drastically strains the operation.

Teams at Work 9: Berlin Airlift, "Operations Vittles and Plainfare"

The Berlin blockade . . . was one of the first major international crises of the Cold War. During the multinational occupation of post–World War II Germany, the Soviet Union blocked the Western Allies' railway, road and canal access to the sectors of Berlin under Allied control. Their aim was to force the western powers to allow the Soviet zone to start supplying Berlin with food and fuel, thereby giving the Soviets practical control over the entire city.

In response, the Western Allies organized the Berlin airlift to carry supplies to the people in West Berlin. . . . The United States Air Force [and] the British Royal Air Force . . . flew over 200,000 flights in one year, providing up to 4,700 tons of daily necessities such as fuel and food to the Berliners. . . .

At the time [of the airlift], West Berlin had 36 days' worth of food, and 45 days' worth of coal. . . .

In total the USA . . . and the RAF . . . delivered 2,326,406 tons, nearly two-thirds of which was coal, on 278,228 flights to Berlin. . . . A total of 101 fatalities were recorded as a result of the operation, including 40 Britons and 31 Americans, mostly due to crashes. Seventeen American and eight British aircraft crashed during the operation. The cost of the Airlift was approximately $224 million.

The Blockade also helped to overcome any remaining differences between the French, British and Americans regarding West Germany, leading to a merger of all three countries' occupation zones into "trizonia." . . . Animosities between Germans and the western Allies, Britain, France and the United States, were greatly reduced by the airlift, with the former enemies recognizing common interests, shared values and mutual respect.

In an amazing display of teamwork, four seemingly different countries with completely distinct morals and ways of life came together to help a nation in need. Had it not been for this unlikely but forged alliance among these countries, the people in West Berlin would have suffered imminent death from starvation and harsh weather conditions. However, this multinational commitment of teamwork ended up being a lifesaver. (From "Berlin Blockade," *Wikipedia*, January 29, 2013.)

Reaping the Rewards

There is little doubt that this shift in your organization and your attitude toward team members will take a great deal of time and effort. But with this time and effort come enormous benefits in terms of the development and maximization of team success. In fact, I am confident that happier and more invested employees will result in stronger sales, better products, and higher levels of success.

Bruce Tulgan said,

> *Leadership is best able to help members anticipate relationship dynamics that are likely to cause conflict and help them prepare for those situations. When I speak to companies, teams, and organizations, I indicate they have two choices. They can either spend time, money, manpower, and resources trying to clean up the problems that result from a lack of proper development training of the team, or they can use those same things to move forward toward the accomplishment of their goals and stated mission. It's usually one or the other. The former puts a strain on the organization to accomplish its most basic functions and tasks. The latter moves the entire team in a positive direction toward mission accomplishment. Management and leadership have to make a choice as to what they'd rather do.*

The reward of strong leadership is the efficient use of time and resources, promoting unity of effort, eliminating duplication of tasks, maximizing available talent, encouraging innovation, and retaining trained and developed talent. There is no way around this. Either you invest in your current employees, or you will have to invest in new ones. The reason why there is so much turnover in the current business environment is not because employees are always looking for greener pastures, but rather because the current pastures are not green enough. As a leader, it is your responsibility to create a nurturing environment that is superfocused on cultivating skills and talent.

There is a common misconception that the best teams in the NFL are those that draft the best players. That is simply incorrect. In reality, the most successful franchises of our time are those that draft well, but, more important, also develop talent. Through a proven method of maximizing talent, teams can spend less money on the front end and create a relationship with their players that instills in them a sense of duty and responsibility to one another. Then, and only then, will championships be won. The same is true in business. Human nature dictates that people want to be motivated, inspired, taught, and developed. But it is up to you to be the driving force and develop the grit to be that type of leader.

CHAPTER 4

THE PLACEMENT: FINDING THE RIGHT FIT

We have all heard the saying about square pegs and round holes. But even though the foolishness of trying to fit something where it does not go is such a common notion, at some point almost every business will find that it has employees who are amazingly talented, but who simply do not fit within the overall scheme and mission of the company. You may even have maximized the talent of fantastic employees, but still feel as if their position in your business is limiting their overall potential. This chapter will offer you compelling lessons and tips to figure out where people fit in your business and how you can reshape job responsibilities to suit your talent. Too many leaders throw out the baby with the bathwater because they have trouble fitting a square peg into a round hole, but that does not have to be the case.

On many levels, finding the right fit for new hires is imperative for the overall productivity of your business. This starts with understanding the essential tools that will help you place talent, one of the most crucial and vital skills that a leader must master to ensure that the right people are doing the right job. The best leaders understand the importance of filling the gaps and finding the missing pieces. At the end of the day, success is a people business, and finding the right fit will help the people on top piece the puzzle together through a three-step process: identify the need, evaluate the talent available, and procure the right fit for your business needs, all the while cross-checking employees' skill sets against your individualized opinions and company requirements.

Finding the right fit means different things to different leaders. For example, Jon Semcken, vice president of Majestic Realty Co., told me, "When identifying the right fit for our company, we choose to hire people that are smarter than us; know more than we do; make us look better; people that are goal-oriented; and those that are loyal to the company and its mission." No matter what it means to you, there is endless value in finding the right fit for your particular business.

Henry Ford said, "Coming together is a beginning. Keeping together is progress. Working together is success." To ensure that the members of your team can work together as one dedicated unit, they must fit not just with one another, but within each other. A team is a like a puzzle or a chain. The pieces have to connect by fitting together, rather than just being stacked on top of one another. If your team members do not fit, your team will never be complete.

After reading this chapter, you will be able to effectively maximize the potential of members through giving them proper responsibilities and understanding roles and responsibilities, understanding the value of crossover opportunities for those showing skills in areas outside of their expertise, feeling better equipped to create a program of backup training in areas outside of team members' expertise, and providing leadership training and opportunities for those who show the will and the ability to do more.

Finding the Right Fit

As we discussed in the previous chapter, when you are running any business, your ultimate goal is to maximize the output of your employees. To achieve this goal, it is crucial that you find the right fit for your employees. Your employees' fit within your organization should be like a perfectly tailored suit. A suit should be form-fitting but comfortable, and should be individually cut to reflect the needs of the person wearing it. The same should be true of your employees' job responsibilities. If you tailor your jobs to the strengths of your employees and ensure that they feel comfortable and fit appropriately into your business, you will position your team to maximize results and achieve high goals.

In reality, all you have to do is look at the results of a poor fit to understand the positive benefits gained as a result of finding the right fit for team members and employees. Time, money, and effort are no longer wasted by being directed toward the losing cause of trying to cram square pegs into round holes, leading to an inability to reach benchmark goals and mission objectives. There is no worse experience in business than watching the potential of your team slowly unraveling at the seams and having little ability to prevent it. The catastrophic end result can even be the eventual dismantling of the entire group and the dreaded word that no team (regardless of vocation, industry, or sport) wants to hear: rebuilding.

Take the example of the National Football League. The NFL is made up of 32 member clubs, each with 53 active players, 8 practice squad players, a coaching staff, a personnel department, and an operations group charged with putting a competitive product on the field during the season.

Every individual plays a vital role in ensuring that the team is physically capable and mentally prepared to do its job. Job descriptions are specific, detailed, and very much specialized. From the assistant equipment manager to the player who holds the ball on field goal attempts, each and every individual must maintain the mental and physical skills and capabilities required to execute his responsibilities.

The head coach and his staff are charged with utilizing the athletic prowess of the players to move the ball down the field efficiently, prevent the opponent from scoring, and ultimately score the most points in order to win the game and move forward toward a Super Bowl Championship.

With that in mind, most football fans realize that it would be ludicrous to ask a wide receiver to play a position that he is unfamiliar with or unqualified to play. First, because of the physical makeup and size of the different players, coaches won't be able to rely upon these team members to execute the plays properly, resulting in poor performance and usually a losing effort.

Second, coaches will begin to see mounting frustration on the part of the player who is working outside of his comfort zone. This often results in attitude changes, temper outbursts, poor work habits, and an overall demeanor that is out of character for the individual.

Finally, the team will begin to question the competency of the coaching staff and front office personnel for blatantly putting the player in a "no win" scenario. It's usually the other team members who notice the poor fit before anyone else does. The team begins to question the organization's commitment to carrying out its well-conceived and well-publicized mission statement. The "ripple effect" of compromising even one employee can lead to an avalanche of poor performance.

The NFL is a business just like any other organization. Among its additional objectives, the goal is to turn a profit and maximize income. When it does so, management, employees, and players all benefit. Herein lies the value of finding the right fit for each employee. This system will effectively and efficiently utilize your personnel resources and maximize their skills, motivating them to produce above and beyond their own realized capabilities because of the satisfaction they gain from a productive contribution toward the good of the team.

It's no different in football or in business. You can go out and identify, hire, and train the best and the brightest, but if these people are placed in the wrong positions, you might as well be hiring incompetent malcontents. Their frustration, lack of production, and eventual sour attitude will lead to losing those employees with good character and to sloppy and poor performance on the part of the employees that remain.

To meet team and personal goals, employees must be given the maximum opportunity to do so, and that goes with being placed in the right roles within the team's operations based on skill sets. By emphasizing these roles and the subsequent training required to enable team members to fully master the associated responsibilities, the organization will see employees as assets to the team and will be willing to take the necessary steps and spend the corresponding resources required to ensure that they fulfill their potential. Through this investment, you as a team leader should expect reciprocation through the elevation of high standards of production and fulfillment of job responsibilities.

Coach Tom Osborne told me,

> When recruiting a team, the process was actually antithetical to how a team plays. When recruited, players are often told how good they are, how important they are, and that they are going to come in and play right away. Leaders say whatever they need to say to get the new member. So, when that process plays out, sometimes you have a player whose mindset isn't necessarily oriented toward team accomplishments, but geared toward individual success. So one thing we tried to do during the recruiting process was to never promise anything other than an opportunity. We never told the player he would be the star or get a certain amount of playing time—those were earned. As a result, we lost some good potential talent, but I think for the most part we probably lost the ones who would have hurt us more than they helped us. And the ones that came here, did so with no expectations other than the opportunity to be part of something special.

The same is true when recruiting and hiring for business teams. Securing the right talent with corresponding attitudes is imperative for building a strong team. Even one bad apple can spoil the barrel. Though finding the right fit for team members seems to take second place to the overall mission, that couldn't be farther from the truth. Fit operates in conjunction with everything that has been discussed to this point, including finding talent, defining the mission, developing skills, and then placing people accordingly. Without the right type of experienced and insightful leadership, many a good team effort and intentions can end up on the losing end of the score.

Teams at Work 10: The Bill & Melinda Gates Foundation (B&MGF)

Bill and Melinda Gates founded "the largest transparently operated private foundation in the world" and fueled it with a $37.4 billion endowment.

It is "driven by the interests and passions of the Gates family." The primary aims of the foundation are, globally, to enhance healthcare and reduce extreme poverty, and in America, to expand educational opportunities and access to information technology. The foundation . . . is controlled by its three trustees: Bill Gates, Melinda Gates and Warren Buffett. . . . The scale of the foundation and the way it seeks to apply business techniques to giving makes it one of the leaders in the philanthrocapitalism revolution in global philanthropy. . . . In 2007, its founders were ranked as the second most generous philanthropists in America.

In 1994, the foundation was formed as the William H. Gates Foundation with an initial stock gift of $94 million. In 1999, [it] was renamed the Bill & Melinda Gates Foundation. . . . On June 25, 2006, Warren Buffett (then the world's richest person . . .) pledged to give the foundation approximately 10 million Berkshire Hathaway Class B shares spread over multiple years through annual contributions, worth approximately $1.5 billion for the year 2006. . . . "Buffett's gift came with three conditions for the Gates foundation: Bill or Melinda Gates must be alive and active in its administration; it must continue to qualify as a charity; and each year it must give away an amount equal to the previous year's Berkshire gift, plus another 5 percent of net assets. Buffett gave the foundation two years to abide by the third requirement."

In 2010, Bill Gates and Warren Buffett took their mission one step further, creating "the Giving Pledge."

"The Giving Pledge" is a campaign to encourage the wealthiest men and women in America to give donate most of their wealth [to charity]. . . . The donation can happen either during the lifetime or after the death of the donor.

To date, more than 81 billionaires have committed to give at least half of their fortune to charity. This accounts for billions of dollars in charitable contributions. One man or woman cannot change the world, but the Giving Pledge shows that a team of billionaires working together certainly can. (From "Bill & Melinda Gates Foundation," *Wikipedia*, January 24, 2013, and "The Giving Pledge," *Wikipedia*, January 10, 2013.)

Three Steps to Success

You should now understand the value of finding the right fit—it can make or break your business. But actually finding the right fit for your team's open positions is easier said than done. If it were simple, there would be no turnover, no firings, and no loss of time and resources. But all of these critical issues stifle business growth day in and day out. However, through building and rebuilding teams year in and year out, it became clear to me that there are specific steps that any leader can take to ensure that she is hiring the right person for the job and positioning the new hire to optimize performance.

Step 1: Identify the need.

Step 2: Evaluate the talent.

Step 3: Procure the desired outcome.

In sports or in business, finding the right fit when building top teams requires a bit more thought then just taking on all challengers for the part. Leaders must have a thorough working knowledge of the team's overall mission and a firm grasp of the requirements of the individual position in question as it relates directly to implementing systems or procedures to achieve mission success.

Leaders should understand the skills necessary for the individual in the position to execute the requirements for that position in a timely, productive, and efficient manner, usually at a high degree of standard. It also becomes incumbent upon the team leaders or those who are making the selection and placement of team members to recognize whether or not a person has the ability to learn, develop, and grow into the position through developmental training programs devised to teach those skills needed to execute the responsibilities of the position.

So let's take the time to study this three-step process to ensure the proper placement of team members and creation of the right fit.

Step 1: Identify the Need

The first step in finding the right fit for your team is understanding and identifying your needs. Don't confuse this with critical factors and position specifics, both of which we spoke about earlier. Those two elements help define the type of team member you're looking for to fulfill the requirements and meet your need. Here, we are focused on the job description, not the skills required to carry out the job.

In previous chapters, when talking about hiring, we spoke about tips and guidance that you can integrate into your hiring practices to find the most talented candidates. Through identifying a need, you take this one step further by ensuring that these talented individuals are good fits for your organization. You can hire the most qualified candidate on the planet, but if he does not fit with your needs and job requirements, it will be for nothing.

For example, a newly formed business needs salespeople to create leads and sell its product. This position calls for a certain type of person with a very special skill set, including persistence, determination, communicative ability, familiarity with the product, and salesmanship. To be a strong salesperson, the employee needs certain position specifics that have historically proved to be commonalities among successful salespeople.

When identifying a need for your business, it's extremely important that you define the task and answer the question: what do you need from this particular position in order to execute your processes focused on achieving your mission? You should find the answer to this question before you begin hiring.

You might notice that there's a lot of predetermined "defining" required of top team leaders before they ever set out to build a successful team. Arguably, this is the first step you should take when identifying your needs. Those leaders who don't bother to take the time to carry out this critical step in the team-building process will be frustrated by their lack of success and their need to constantly replace team members.

With this in mind, what separates the very best team leaders from the rest of the pack is the ability to identify and find the "missing pieces" for their team or business. Doing a self-assessment and asking questions like, "What role or individual are we lacking to complete our efforts?" and "What and where is that last cog in the machine?" will help steer you in the right direction.

Think about it. You've established evaluative criteria to hire the best and the brightest, set a clear-cut mission statement with well-defined benchmark goals, worked to develop your team members to maximize their skills, and done everything necessary to establish a winning culture and an effective team environment, yet you still can't seem to reach productive success.

Sometimes the addition of one particular skill or individual can act as the catalyst to take the rest of the team to the top. Remember those cartoons from your childhood? The ones where the Coyote chased the Road Runner time and time again? Even though the Road Runner was faster and smarter, the Coyote would always stay close, often by strapping on a jet pack to propel him forward. The same is true with your organization's catalysts. These hires supercharge your productivity and help you achieve your desired results faster. Without that jet pack, the Coyote would not even come close to catching the Road Runner, and without your strategically positioned company catalysts, you will plod along at a snaillike pace.

It's important that you study and scout the competition, and know what it takes to be successful in your realm of business. As you look to rebuild or add to your own team's culture, be open to people who come into your scenario as outsiders. They bring past experience and understanding of systems to reach particular mission goals, and you should look to add those pieces that might fit with your own.

One last, but simple analogy might be that of baking a cake. You may have all the necessary ingredients (flour, eggs, sugar, water, and flavoring), but without heat and time, it's just a conglomeration of goop. The heat is your catalyst, and it provides the necessary jump to bring it all together. So ask yourself, is there something missing from your own recipe?

Through identifying the need, you should be able to answer these simple yet imperative questions:

What skill set and background are needed to excel in my organization's open position?

What will be the day-to-day responsibilities of my new hire?

What is the job description for my open position?

When you have answered these questions, you will feel focused and concentrated on the position for which you are hiring. This will prevent distractions or the hiring of talented but incorrectly placed employees.

Step 2: Evaluate the Talent

Once you have evaluated the need and defined the type of team member you are searching for, the next step is finding great team members with the flexibility to produce in numerous facets of team operations. The first consideration you should study when evaluating the talent for specific positions is defining exactly the type of person you are searching for. To make this distinction easier, it is best to break down this large pool into two classes: those with experience and those who are fresh into the real world.

When you are recruiting more experienced employees, their extensive and varied résumés will bring different understandings and perspectives that can be gained only through time and practice. Usually these types of team members are older, more seasoned, and looked upon as veterans of their industry or cause.

The younger, less experienced teammates may have schooling or training in their background that can lead to responsibilities other than those of their primary positions as well. In the evaluation process, look for those team members who show the potential for multitasking and who have mastered their frontline tasks to date. Finding the best fit requires thought and effort. By evaluating the talent pool with the directed purpose of creating a specific type of culture in mind, you should find it easier to manage this difficult task.

Age is a vital consideration for any organization and its team members, but it is not the only one. Another valuable means of fashioning the best fit for your organization is to maintain an intimate understanding of specific job descriptions and requirements. If you have a thorough awareness of the skills needed to perform each open position, you can better assess the talent to find the most logical fit. If you do not understand the bounds within which you are working, you will find it next to impossible to achieve your desired goals.

The purpose of evaluating the talent is to determine whether a talented and well-trained candidate fits your job requirements. Identifying the need focuses on understanding both the open position and its requirements, whereas evaluating the talent helps to determine which of the gifted individuals fit the best into both the open position and the organization.

Michael Evans is a winemaker in Argentina. In December 2004, Evans went to Mendoza for a long weekend of wine tasting, and he never left. The magic and majesty of Mendoza, along with his chance meeting with cofounder Pablo Gimenez Riili, resulted in the creation of the Vines of Mendoza in the spring of 2005. This company makes Argentine wines, owns vineyards, and provides luxury residence ownership and winemaking that are accessible to wine lovers worldwide.

Four times a year, the company delivers Argentina's best boutique wines directly to your door—handpicked wines that are otherwise nearly impossible to find outside of Argentina. One year after the launch of the Wine Club, it opened the Vines of Mendoza Tasting Room and Blending Lab in the heart of Mendoza's city center. It is the first space in Argentina dedicated solely to showcasing Argentine wines.

Winemaking is dependent upon the correct balance and perfect fit of team members. Michael Evans told me, "We evaluate employees based on their professional abilities, but also their ability to fit within our organization. Team fit and great attitudes are the most important attributes for our staff. Often, someone may be perfect on paper, but if that person doesn't fit our company personality, he rarely is a good fit for the organization."

By evaluating the talent, you should be able to answer these simple yet imperative questions:

Which of these talented candidates will be the best fit for my open job?

Which of these talented candidates will help improve the culture of my company?

Who will be strongest catalyst for my mission and propel my company to the next level?

When you have answered these questions, you will be better positioned to review the best and the brightest candidates and make a difficult decision for the overall business of the organization. There may be no wrong answer when it comes to qualified new hires, but there will certainly be a better opportunity and a more accurate fit.

Step 3: Procure the Desired Outcome

The final step in finding the right fit is to procure the desired outcome. At some point, you have to make a decision. Frequently it may seem impossible for you to find an individual with all the aspects you're looking for to fill a position and immediately execute the task required to accomplish the mission. But if you start with the best and the brightest and then ensure that you haven't hired a running back to do a quarterback's responsibilities, you'll find that you reach your desired outcome more often than not.

If you do not achieve your desired outcome, the well-thought-out work that you did in identifying your need and evaluating the talent was wasted. The end will justify the means and will always remain as the equalizer and measuring stick for your hires and decisions. Procuring your desired outcome requires forward thinking and a laserlike focus on the inevitable goal.

If you choose to use technology, resources, or other available measures to procure the right fit, it is essential that you identify both your desired outcome and the best way to achieve it. It is just like a science experiment. You need to create a thesis for your experiment and begin to take the appropriate steps to reach that result. Before you begin any job search, you should have a clear and concise mission. Only then can you procure the desired outcome and confirm that you're headed in the right direction.

When it comes to using technology, there are numerous resources available to help you accomplish this task. One of these, Eye-Scout, LLC, produces ways of finding the right fit using Department of Defense technologies and mathematical algorithms that create equations that can weigh the position-specific factors according to your team's needs at a specific position. The Eye-Scout product then looks at the various factors and splits the hairs among the prospects. You must know what you absolutely can't live without and what you would be willing to compromise on for the position in question.

By procuring the desired outcome, you should be able to review your decision and answer these simple yet imperative questions:

> Does my specific hire fit within the previously created mission statement for my organization?
>
> After six months, was my new hire the right fit for the open position?
>
> After one year, would I have made the same hiring decision for the job opening?

By acknowledging the answers to these questions, you can learn from your mistakes and ensure that your hiring practices procure the correct fit over and over again.

The Culmination of Hard Work

If they are done correctly, the three steps every leader should take to find the right fit will ultimately culminate in a powerful and effective team that pushes the organization forward during both periods of prosperity and difficult times. After executing this process, you will be well situated to understand the requirements and needs of positions as they relate directly to the overall mission. It is no secret that truly great teams have already reviewed the finer details and laid out plans and procedures as a result of this process, and now so can you. This can take some time up front, but it will pay off tenfold on the back end.

The best way to know your expensive sports car is to take it apart, piece by piece, and then put it all back together again. You'll then know exactly how each system acts with the others and in conjunction with the entire vehicle to allow the car to accelerate down the road at breakneck speeds! You'll see where you can drop unneeded weight that might be slowing you down, and perhaps identify areas where you can make aftermarket enhancements to increase your efficiency. The purpose of identifying the need, evaluating the talent, and procuring the desired outcome is to disassemble and reassemble the core of your organization—your team. By achieving an intimate awareness of your team, you can then make the proper adjustments to perfect it and maximize its performance.

You should constantly review who your team is and why it exists. Dig into what your sole purpose is as a mission and whether the benchmark goals truly point toward achieving this mission or are just place setters to trick you into thinking you've reached your purpose. Instead of trying to "go with your gut" to hire and place team members in a successful manner, you'll have constructed a framework that can't help but lead you directly to the right individuals for the right jobs within your organization.

Cross-Training

To this point, we have discussed how to optimize team members for specific positions within your business. However, one of the most effective and strategic steps that the best leaders take during their hiring practices is to hire for breadth and latitude. This means that, when making employment decisions, you should always consider the crossover potential for any employee. You may hire for a particular vacancy, but you would be wise to reflect on the possibility of growth and an increase in this person's responsibilities.

Those in today's new generation of team members are more adept at spreading their wings outside of their primary responsibility. If a team leader expects one of her members to take the extra steps required for crossover training while remaining excited about the opportunity that this gives her own career, you must be willing to provide motivation and rewards for doing more than required. This will keep team members motivated and at ease with their newfound accountability.

Today's teams are überfocused on being trim and "lean and mean." Team members are often asked to do even more toward fulfilling the mission accomplishments, in some instances doing two or three jobs at once. So, it's important to focus on hiring team members with the skills to perform or the ability to learn multiple tasks directed toward the organization's goals and then empowering them to perform those tasks.

Coach Tom Osborne told me,

> *When I became a member of Congress, I had roughly eighteen people working for me, a staff of eight or nine in Washington, and another eight or nine people in Nebraska and the district offices. One thing I noticed early on was that people would not take responsibility and were somewhat paralyzed in their job duties because their leader had previously monitored them very closely. As a result, I felt we were wasting a lot of time and energy, and handicapping our people, who were all hired because of their qualifications. I began to empower them and give them more authority to act on their own and do what they thought*

needed to be done to serve the people in the Third District. As a result, I think we were able to do a lot more. People were better trained and qualified to perform well outside of their job descriptions.

We tried to make sure that it wasn't all top down, that people were given a responsibility and a job to do, and the resources and freedom to do it. With this structure, their talents began to appear, and their productiveness and energy increased exponentially once we began to get the idea across. They had a role to play, and they were given a lot of autonomy within that role.

For the individual team member's developmental growth, this provides a conduit for a broader understanding and acceptance of other areas and aspects of the entire process. It also allows the team member to have a varied perspective and an opportunity for creativity within the same team environment. From the perspective of the leaders, having employees who have the knowledge and ability to execute various tasks gives greater flexibility in problem solving within operations. It provides quick options in emergency situations and can be a more efficient way of using resources throughout the organization.

As crucial as hiring employees with crossover potential is to team success, remember that forcing team members to perform multiple roles for a long period of time can stretch them too thin and lead to job burnout, which gives the same negative ripple effect as placing an employee in the wrong position initially. You're better off training and developing team members to take on backup roles for personal growth and team crisis management, not to squeeze another drop out of them as a commodity. Believe me, great team members recognize the difference between being utilized as an asset to the operation and being used up as a commodity in the process.

Backing Up the Talent

Cross-training offers the unique and exciting possibility of new hires becoming valuable assets to the organization by becoming better trained and more capable. If a balanced chord is struck, employees see greater opportunity and employers build stronger teams. But it does not stop there. Modern-day hiring practices should focus not just on crossing over the talent, but also on backing it up. In business, life happens. People get sick, resign, get fired, get pregnant, take vacations, and even retire. And with them go their ability to perform some of the daily tasks that must be carried out.

The famous boxer Joe Frazier said, "You can map out a fight plan or a life plan, but when the action starts, it may not go the way you planned, and you're down to your reflexes. That's where your roadwork shows. If you cheated on that in the dark of the morning, well, you're going to get found out now, under the bright lights."

In business, preparation means everything. As long as everything goes according to plan, your bumps in the road will be small. However, when life happens, your preparation (or lack thereof) will stand front and center. What happens when your IT guy falls off his bike and has to take weeks of medical leave? Obviously, your systems crash the next day. But then what? You are sitting in your office with a major emergency on your hands and no one available to deal with the problem. You can outsource, bring in a specialized IT contractor, or try to fix the system yourself. Any of these options will almost always end with the loss of time and resources, and that is the best-case scenario. But things do not have to play out this way.

Life doesn't seem to slow down in any capacity, especially when you're focused on achieving a specific mission and using benchmarks as points along the path. In the blink of an eye, an NFL season can start with great promise and be lost to inconsistency and frustration in only a few short weeks.

There are similar situations in business: the pursuit of big contracts, seasonal sales targets, and quarterly reports. Where is there the time to train existing team members or employees to master not only their own responsibilities, but those in a backup capacity as well?

This is a very difficult and arduous task for any team leader, yet it is one that is vital in dealing with the unexpected twists and turns that will inevitably face your business. More often than not, you're hiring to fill a particular position to meet an immediate requirement or need, and you must train that new hire for the position in question.

However, the scenario described earlier happens far too often, and leaders should consider this conundrum when making hiring decisions. Every business needs a backup plan, and both your hiring procedures and your training methods should reflect this notion. This is done through proper training, but also through identifying on the front end those candidates who may major in one area of skills but minor in another. Once they are hired, show your employees that you have confidence that they can handle emergency and backup tasks, give them a sense of ownership in the operational process, and display your willingness to take them to the next level through development. This can be done quickly through more extensive training, situational exercises, and/or "riding sidecar" and shadowing the primary team member in an "on-the-job" scenario.

It takes a very confident and committed leader to train a team member in a backup position, but when life happens, you will find that the small amount of time invested in this training can save you hours, if not days, of time on the back end.

Teams at Work 11: New York Philharmonic (Philharmonic-Symphony Society of New York)

[This group is] a symphony orchestra based in New York City. . . . Organized in 1842, The orchestra is older than any other extant American symphonic institution by nearly four decades; its record-setting 14,000th concert was given in December 2004. . . .

The orchestra was founded by the American-born conductor Ureli Corelli Hill in 1842, with the aid of the then famous and feted Irish composer William Vincent Wallace. . . . The first concert of the New York Philharmonic took place on December 7, 1842. . . .

In 1921 the Philharmonic merged with New York's National Symphony Orchestra. . . . The year 1928 marked the New York Philharmonic's last and most important merger: with the New York Symphony Society. The Symphony had been quite innovative in its 50 years prior to the merger. It made its first domestic tour in 1882, introduced educational concerts for young people in 1891, and gave the premieres of works such as Gershwin's Concerto in F and Holst's Egdon Heath. The merger of these two venerable institutions consolidated extraordinary financial and musical resources. . . .

The Philharmonic performed in Pyongyang at the invitation of the North Korean government on February 26, 2008. . . . In response to initial criticism of performing a concert limited to the privileged elite, the New York Philharmonic arranged for the concert to be broadcast live on North Korean television and radio. It was additionally broadcast live on CNN and CNN International.

The New York Philharmonic has garnered 19 Grammy Awards under 6 different music directors.

As accomplished as this orchestra has been over the years, the most amazing aspect of its history is why it has achieved such unparalleled success. More than any other type of performing arts organization, an orchestra requires a perfectly harmonious team working together in an interwoven and intricately intertwined manner to produce a perfect result. Even one off note by one team member can cause devastating and catastrophic results. The teamwork displayed by any orchestra is inspiring, but the New York Philharmonic enlists some of the most talented team members in the world. It is not just about being a fantastic musician; it is also about being a harmonious member of the team. The result is not just amazing, but also award winning. (From "New York Philharmonic," *Wikipedia*, December 30, 2012.)

Square Pegs, Round Holes

Identifying, evaluating, procuring, cross-training, and backing up—we have discussed them all. But even with all of these options available to you and your organization, sometimes you'll find talented people who just don't end up fitting the position they were brought in for, but who are also too good to let go.

In this position, what does a strong leader do?

This is an often overlooked aspect of finding the right fit for team members, because when the initial plan goes awry, leaders tend to "throw out the baby with the bathwater." But this does not have to be the case. Most square pegs can be repositioned and remolded into productive members of your business. Albert Einstein said, "If the facts don't fit the theory, change the facts."

It starts with recalling that you added this particular member because of his critical factor makeup and skills that seemed congruent with another position. He passed a sort of vetting process just to get to the point that you're at now. Unless he's displayed qualities that were unknown to you and are contrary to your overall efforts toward the mission, then there might be something salvageable, and perhaps hidden, that can be of value to another area of the business.

But first, you might be willing to change the requirements of the position a bit, perhaps by altering the system that works toward meeting your goals. You don't have to compromise the bottom line; you just have to consider changing the manner in which you go about reaching it in order to take full advantage of the strengths that a particularly unusual team member might provide.

Author Bruce Tulgan told me,

If somebody is not playing their role properly or up to expectations, as a leader, you have to find out what is going wrong. But the flipside of that is, it offers an opportunity to try to match an individual's strengths and inclinations with a task or responsibility. But what you can do is to try to find out what is somebody's strength or inclination and map that into their area of responsibility. Usually the issue arises when there's a mismatch and people feel like it's not going well. You then have to figure out what's going wrong here. If you can't lift a box, you can't work in the warehouse. So the solution is to find different paths for the person or a different role, and if you can't do that for them, then they just don't fit. They may need more tools, techniques, and/ or information. There is a possibility they have the skill and knowledge to do the job, but are not motivated for one reason or another. Leaders must then reflect whether they are providing clear expectations and support or setting the employee up for success. If the person doesn't have the talent, then change the role or the person.

Leaders at the very top usually have the task of ensuring the accomplishment of this mission, but unless this is set in stone by an unyielding management, why not think outside the box and take a different path or tweak a particular system? This shows the employee her unique value to the group, while demonstrating to the rest of the team the organization's flexibility of thought when it comes to achieving the most important aspect—the mission.

But be certain of this member's strengths before you change the entire system and "ripple" other members; if you don't, the rest of the team may quickly see this as preferring "favoritism" to mission accomplishment.

If you've done your work on the critical factors and position specifics thoroughly, and have instituted a weighted requirements evaluation process, you can look at the perceived strengths and/or real weaknesses of the member and place him in a position that is more congruent with the skill set that he's shown through his evaluation, his initial attempts at his primary position, or your own past experience.

But remember that not all employees can be salvaged. Sometimes an employee is the wrong fit. You should never give up easily, but there comes a point of diminished returns. Once you have invested all you have into an employee but still see little, if any, improvement, be confident in your decision to move on. Ultimately, this will be better for both you and your former colleague. This chapter has given you the skills to find the perfect fit for employees, and also how to ensure that employees are well trained and can step in when the going gets tough. But with this in mind, never forget that sometimes saying good-bye is the best thing for everyone involved.

Fuel the Fire

As a leader, it is your job to continue shoveling the coal so that the engine keeps turning. It is not about hiring and firing, but about doing so in a strategic and calculated manner. Anyone can offer a candidate the job, but only a select and shrinking group of people can lead in a manner that inculcates smart and intentional hiring practices.

Consider the tale about the doctor and his mechanic. A heart surgeon took his car to his local garage for a regular service, where he usually exchanged a little friendly banter with the owner, a skilled but not especially wealthy mechanic.

"So tell me," said the mechanic, "I've been wondering about what we both do for a living, and how much more you get paid than me."

"Yes?" said the surgeon.

"Well look at this," said the mechanic as he worked on a big, complicated engine. "I check how it's running, open it up, fix the valves, and put it all back together so it works good as new. We basically do the same job don't we? And yet you are paid ten times what I am—how do you explain that?"

The surgeon thought for a moment, smiling gently, and replied, "Try doing your job with the engine running." (Taken from http://www.businessballs.com/stories.htm#speed_camera_story.)

Leadership is a fluid, ongoing process that occurs at the speed of light. You cannot switch off the machine while you fine-tune its parts and perfect its operation. Everything happens with the engine on. Thus, by finding the right fit, training people for multiple positions and strengths, and backing up the talent, you position your organization to constantly evolve and fix itself without having to pull the plug on the goal of moving forward in a meaningful and successful manner.

Teams at Work 12: Medical Teamwork (Facial Transplant Surgery)

Richard Norris was 22 when a gun accident took his lips, his nose and the front portion of his tongue. The damage to his jaw left him with limited mouth mobility and gave the appearance that his face had sunken into itself. . . .

For 15 years, Norris, of Hillsville, Va., hid behind a surgical mask. He avoided eating in public and shopped for groceries at night. He lived as a "recluse," according to doctors, "not a functioning member of society."

[Then] Norris, 37, underwent a 36-hour surgery lauded as the most extensive face transplant in history. Three days later, he looked in the mirror. He had a nose. He could move his tongue. He would no longer need a mask. [A week later, he was able to brush his teeth and shave.]

The operation, which took place March 19 and 20, 2012, at Maryland Shock Trauma Center, was the Baltimore hospital's first full face transplant. It included replacing the tongue, teeth, and upper and lower jaws, all from one anonymous donor. . . .

The operation was the culmination of a decade's worth of research funded by the Office of Naval Research as part of an effort to expand facial reconstruction possibilities for troops injured by makeshift bombs.

Many developments in Baltimore have been made possible by the U.S. Defense Department, which has provided this funding for face and hand operations for wounded soldiers.

The results of countless team meetings, conference calls, and practice on cadavers were put to the test during the marathon surgery [on Norris. The procedure] involved more than 150 doctors, nurses, and UMMC staff members as part of a remarkable 36-hour surgery.

Surgeons also transplanted a heart, lungs, a liver, and a kidney from the same anonymous donor, to other patients.

It took hundreds of team members and thousands of hours of practice to successfully rebuild the patient's face. The team of doctors and nurses that actually participated in the surgery worked together in an amazing way. The smallest slip of the hand could have caused terrible results and even death. However, the team worked as one and, through its flawless work, had Norris saying, "People used to stare at me because of my disfigurement. Now they can stare at me in amazement and in the transformation I have made. I am now able to walk past people and no one even gives me a second look."

(From Maggie Fazeli Fard, "Face Transplant for Virginia Man Is Lauded as Most Extensive in History," *Washington Post*, March 27, 2012.)

CHAPTER 5

THE EXECUTION: THE Xs AND Os OF TEAM SUCCESS

The talent has been secured, the mission is clear, and the pieces of the puzzle have all been laid out on the table, each in its own comfortable and thought-out place to ensure that the fit is right. But now it is time to begin executing the game plan. Here, we are talking about performance. American actress Mae West said, "An ounce of performance is worth pounds of promises." Just like any NFL team, you can have all the talent in the world, but if you do not communicate your goals to your players and make a strong point of execution, you will fall flat. This chapter will give you everything you need to know to improve your execution, from effective communication techniques, to building a direct and executable strategy, to understanding exactly what makes a team tick.

We will take an in-depth look at how you can delegate the power to influence and motivate upper management in a meaningful way while ensuring that the trickle-down effect is potent and consistent. Creating an environment for team success is just as important as developing the actual team, and this chapter will give readers a compelling system to implement into a company that guarantees the creation of a nurturing and flourishing environment for all employees alike. Many leaders have trouble relating to their team members because of the generation gap and the "new" breed of employees, leading to inefficient and ineffective practices across the board. By understanding these potential pitfalls, leaders can create a game plan that is sure to boost their business to an atmosphere of achievement.

After reading this chapter, you will have a better understanding of how to create a positive environment that allows every department to review and report on the details of its operations; take full and strategic advantage of information technology to communicate; rely on experts to supplement the team's work; analyze, compare, and contrast your team with competitors in your industry; create constant, accurate, and detailed financial feedback; think outside the box and constantly work toward improvements in plans and systems; build a system that allows for multiple inputs from all angles of the organization; and reach out to the history of the organization, embracing past accomplishments to emphasize team development.

Take a Page from Newton

Most people think that the famous cookie the Fig Newton is named after the celebrated mathematician and thinker Sir Isaac Newton. Actually, Kennedy Biscuit Works created this cookie in 1891 when James Henry Mitchell invented a machine that could mass-produce the delicious biscuit. However, the cookies were named after the Massachusetts town of Newton, which was close to Kennedy Biscuits. Sir Isaac Newton may not have given us a delectable biscuit, but he did give us three very important laws of motion. After watching an apple fall from a tree, Newton developed his laws of motion at the young age of 23. His first law of motion is, "An object at rest will stay at rest unless an unbalanced force acts upon it, while an object in motion will not change velocity unless an unbalanced force acts upon it."

Your business and your game plan behave the same way. As long as the waves are small and the tide is gentle, your business will continue in a meaningful and successful manner. However, when dynamic forces like the economy, competitors, or inner turmoil are present, things change considerably. Therein lies the importance of implementing your game plan—it keeps the ship going in the right direction, even in the face of outside forces. As President Franklin D. Roosevelt put it so aptly, "The only thing we have to fear is fear itself." I say we can plan for everything else.

Your preparation will provide you with flexibility and an avenue for analyzing your efforts toward achieving your mission. The secret of the most outstanding team leaders and their subsequent accomplishments is "less is more." That is, you don't necessarily tell people how to do things as much as you tell them what needs to be done.

Standardize Your Approach

The first step in executing your game plan is standardizing it for your company. During my years in the Air Force, I learned the value and importance of regulation manuals, or "Reg Books," for standardizing and guiding operations regardless of personnel or working environment. In the "Regs" were the requirements for accomplishing the mission, baseline standards, and procedures that could be constantly used as references to ensure unity and stability of efforts. These Regs were meant to be a road map that team leaders and personnel could use as a guideline for accomplishing various necessary critical events along the path to the final destination.

The Regs left no question as to what had to be completed and the standards by which the Air Force expected things to be done. I transferred this to the NFL as I began to revamp the Denver Broncos' scouting process in the early 1990s. At that time, most of the directives were passed on to the scouts through midlevel managers in the Personnel Department. Many times the lack of communication was deafening to the scouts in the field: "What am I supposed to do, and how do they want me to do it?" With scouts coming from various positions and backgrounds within college and professional football, evaluation reports were often as varied as 31 flavors of ice cream. You could take your pick, and there was plenty to pick from.

But when a standardized game plan was implemented, not only on the field, but also in the draft room, scouting evaluations suddenly began to focus on the team's needs and requirements. It wasn't my place to tell the scouts what they did or didn't see on the road as they evaluated the top college players, but I could remind them of the minimum requirements necessary to complete the evaluation and "paint the picture" for Bronco decision makers in the draft room.

Now it was easier to compare and contrast various players based on positional needs, round projection, and levels of competition. The process was no longer tainted by individual emotions or bias. The information that was being gathered and analyzed in the schools of the Northeast was the same as the information that was being collected in the Southwest. Scouts were no longer guessing at what the coach or the GM might want during draft meetings, and if they did have a question, they could usually find the answer from the requirements laid down in the "Scouting Bible."

Implementing a Reg Book for your business is not a difficult task, but it takes time and dedication. It should answer questions like:

What's our mission?

How can we go about achieving it?

What is embedded in the fabric of our company that makes us special?

What are the basics of our game plan?

Through answering these questions and creating a Reg Book, you will take your "resting" plan and create the force that puts it into motion.

Teams at Work 13: International Space Station (ISS)—"The Final Frontier"
The ISS serves as a microgravity and space environment research lab in which crew members conduct experiments in biology, human biology, physics, astronomy, meteorology, and other fields. The station is suited for the testing of spacecraft systems and equipment required for missions to the Moon and to Mars.

The ISS . . . is a joint project between five participating space agencies: [those of the United States, Russia, Japan, Canada, and Europe]. The station is divided into two sections, the Russian orbital segment . . . and the United States orbital segment, . . . which is shared by many nations.

[The ISS] has been continuously occupied for [over] 12 years [and is] serviced by Soyuz spacecraft, Progress spacecraft, the Automated Transfer Vehicle, the H-II Transfer Vehicle, and formerly the Space Shuttle. It has been visited by astronauts and cosmonauts from 15 different nations. On 25 May 2012, SpaceX became the world's first privately held company to sent a cargo load, via the Dragon spacecraft, to the International Space Station.

Ownership of modules, station usage by participating nations, and responsibilities for station resupply were established [through an International Treaty signed in 1998].

As of 2010 NASA budgeted $58.7 billion for the station from 1985 to 2015, or $72.4 billion in 2010 dollars. The cost is $150 billion including 36 shuttle flights at $1.4 billion each, Russia's $12 billion ISS budget, Europe's $5 billion, Japan's $5 billion, and Canada's $2 billion. Assuming 20,000 person-days of use from 2000 to 2015 by two to six-person crews, each person-day would cost $7.5 million.

Cooperation revolves around numerous projects and systems within the ISS including cranes and robotic arms, life support, atmospheric control, food, hygiene, power and thermal control, communications and computers, repairs, launching and docking. In March of 2012 the five participants agreed to renew their pledge to maintain ISS through at least 2020.

Assembling the Space Station required 45 launches (36 from the United States and 9 from Russia) and 1,705 hours of space walks, which is double the number of hours that U.S. astronauts have walked in space since the beginning of the space program. The Space Station has 70 separate major components and hundreds of minor ones, all of which were assembled for the first time in space. The construction of the Space Station was a collaboration of 100,000 people, hundreds of companies, and 16 nations spread over four continents: the United States, Russia, Canada, Japan, Belgium, Brazil, Denmark, France, Germany, Italy, the Netherlands, Norway, Spain, Sweden, Switzerland, and the United Kingdom. Talk about global teamwork at its best. (Based on "International Space Station," *Wikipedia*, January 22, 2013.

Aim Straight and Don't Miscommunicate

The Reg Book can provide clarity for your team and your organization, and is a source of communication. It is one of many ways to project your mission and your team goals. While nothing can replace the importance of having a talented and dedicated team dynamic and team leader, it's people that put a resting plan into motion. The cartoonist Walt Kelly first used the quotation "We have met the enemy and he is us" in his strip *Pogo* in 1970. For most teams, the "enemy" is lack of communication. Teams that don't communicate and are not communicated to, whether because of internal turmoil or interference by outside forces, will never succeed. They suffocate through an inability to act and react to other forces that knock them off course.

Author Bruce Tulgan told me,

The best business leaders gravitate to the notion that management needs to be stronger and more engaged, and to spend more time spelling out expectations and communicating, setting up people for success, making sure people know what to do and how to do it, making sure they have the resources they need, and helping people navigate interdependency. Performance needs to be much better in terms of expectations being monitored, measured, and documented more carefully—all through direct communication. It may be very time-consuming, but there is value in convincing people that the way it's happening now will cost you less on the front end than fixing it on the back end. So you're forever helping managers see that it's worth their time to guide, direct, and communicate.

The world today is more connected and more open to various forms of communication than at any previous point in history. Yet it's amazing how quickly the efforts of even the most efficient teams can come to a screeching halt when just a single directive is missed or misinterpreted. British actress Emma Thompson said, "Any problem, big or small, within a family always seems to start with bad communication. Someone isn't listening."

Keeping your team aware and informed in a timely and efficient manner is vital to executing your plan, and thus to the eventual success of your mission. The following are some of the most meaningful ways to engage and lock into your employees.

Face-to-Face Communication

The most effective communication techniques are those that get the message across. The end truly justifies the mean. Communication is most affected by the acronym *TDD*—time, distance, and dissemination. When you communicate, the distance between the communicator and the person receiving the information and the manner in which you communicate play the most important roles in the entire process.

While nothing replaces face-to-face communication, this is becoming a lost art in the techno-savvy world of faster, faster, and faster. Regardless of the size of a team, it's the lack of one-on-one exchanges that has most often brought down the efforts of an entire group. Think about the "ripple effect" of the disgruntled employee who can't figure out why he has to work overtime, the "locker room lawyer" who's upset with the coaching staff because of his lack of playing time, or the young intern griping about being passed over for a promotion. Unless you have your ear to the street and engage in direct communication with your team members, these feelings of chagrin will go unnoticed. If feasible, make it a point to see, hear, and speak with your employees at least once per month. If you are not in a position to do so, ensure that your upper management finds the time to do so.

Set It in Stone

When the communication process lacks clarity, we all fail. When I speak with current and former NFL players, their number one complaint about coaching and front office management is the lack of clear communication regarding just about everything. It's one thing to speak *with* someone and quite another to speak *at* her. Effective team leaders, whether one-on-one, in tactical groups, or with the entire organization, pursue timeliness, restrain from ambiguity, ensure proper feedback of understanding, and are willing to take full advantage of all of today's technologies to get the word out to team members. Because of Newton's "unbalanced forces" and the outside dynamics that can knock even the best-laid plans off course, teams should constantly be reviewing, revising, and updating their written lines of communication.

Create Clear Context

When the individual looks at the overall mission and doesn't have the context for how he fits into that mission, of course the end result seems daunting. We often hear questions like, "How is my little role going to affect the overall process? Will my efforts accomplish anything of magnitude?" The key answer to both these questions is context.

For example, to the untrained fan, the right offensive guard on a football team seems insignificant. Because of his position on the field, he's rarely seen on television. He doesn't carry or catch the ball, so commentators place little emphasis on his play. Offensive guards just fill in the space between the ball and the end of the line of scrimmage.

Yet without the right offensive guard, there would be a seven- to nine-foot gap between two other positions, allowing an opposing player to run through this hole and take down the quarterback. The offense's timing and rhythm would be totally out of synch, and a majority of plays would be over before they ever started—all because one player made a small mistake. Without an effective offense, a football team is probably going to lose. Because of the positional alignment of the entire offensive line, the right offensive guard must secure the interior advances of the defense. His overall context in relation to the offense's execution becomes crystal clear when he is removed from the picture. It seems like a small issue on the front end, but the back-end consequences are insurmountable. So one of the greatest contributions a team leader can convey to the individual is a sense of context in terms of how she relates to the accomplishment of the mission.

Set a Timeline

Providing a timeline in relation to major milestones and significant events can help support the context you're looking to create. The Denver Broncos' Scouting Bible left no questions regarding deadlines and projections because it utilized a detailed calendar of events that could be readily seen by all members of the team. It was a built-in priority system that internally emphasized where team members should focus their own efforts at any given point. Everyone knew what needed to be done in order to take the next step. Everyone also realized that if he didn't carry out his responsibilities, the team couldn't move forward. Understanding the importance of the timeline and the calendar was an internal motivator. Nobody wanted to hold up the group.

In football, you don't just take 22 players, march them out onto the field, throw out the ball, and shout, "Play!" It takes hours and hours of preparation and practice. There are people working behind the scenes to ensure the maximum output of the athletes, people working to safeguard the health and well-being of the players, people evaluating the on-field production and looking for new talent to supplement the team, people devoted to taking care of the team members' families through insurance, payroll, and support programs, and people working to publicize the message that the team wants to express to its fans and to the community. All of this is done in order to win football games, but each member of the team, both on and off the field, must understand where his efforts fit into the overall mission. The same is true in any business.

When President Kennedy challenged the nation to send a man to the moon and bring him safely back within the decade, it was a clear and concise mission statement. But it took years of preparation, successes, and setbacks before NASA realized that dream. What motivated the engineer working on the "escape tower" for the command module? What pushed the dieticians to find better ways of packaging meals for the astronauts? What guided the seamstress working on individual stitches in the space gloves worn during the lunar walk? It was all an understanding of context and how one individual's efforts, or lack thereof, could mean success or failure for the entire mission.

Apple Tree Leadership

The most effective team leaders are able to empower other leaders and managers in a compassionate and assisting sort of way. Communicating that you care is vital to team success. But the reality is that you can do only so much. Great leaders communicate at every level. These leaders give ownership of the mission through allowing power and control at the operational level. General George S. Patton probably put it best when he said, "Never tell people how to do things. Tell them what to do and they will surprise you with their ingenuity." Your team members should be fully aware of the requirements, but they should be given the latitude to execute those requirements in an effective and efficient manner. Midlevel leaders who are empowered with the authority to do just this are force multipliers.

Dr. Stephen Long, president of the Institute for Level Six Leadership, may have the best description of how this works in his Apple Tree vs. Christmas Tree analogy. He told me:

> In essence, we live in a Christmas tree world, in which organizations are shaped like pyramids. Christmas tree organizations are authoritarian and inorganic. Life is good at the top, but toxic intracompetition exists in the middle. Productivity is supposed to come from the bottom,

but it's difficult for people to perform with the weight of the organization on their backs.

In apple tree organizations, leaders occupy the organization's center rather than the top. They inhabit the tree trunk, where they're able to reach up to support producers and middle managers or dig into the roots to access resources. Middle managers are branches moving resources from leaders to producers, working collaboratively and openly with each branch. The producers are at the top, where they get all the resources they need for high performance.

Dr. Long's definition displays the power of delegation, allowing various levels of your team's leadership to convey the vision and successfully keeping them focused on the mission and those aspects that are most important to its completion. That is how you accomplish being everywhere at once. But it takes a TEAM leader who has the energy and drive to communicate, and how he goes about doing this is just as important as when, where, or why. An engaged, enthusiastic, and positive message gets farther with most team members than a top-down directive. Midlevel TEAM leaders need to know that they can count on the top-level leaders for honest and ethical guidance, with a clear foresight of where they want to go.

There is no faster way to lose your team than displaying an inability to be depended upon. Great teams are powered by great decision makers, capable of taking in multiple points of view, contrasting those points to the mission, and then developing a course of action that best meets the needs to accomplish that mission.

It Comes from the Core

It is easy to say that communication comes from the core and from the middle of your organization, but implementing this strategic measure is not nearly as easy. To accomplish this, you have to train your management team to ensure that the trickle-down effect of your vision and mission is potent and consistent. We often hear that success in any organization or team starts at the top with a clear and consistent vision that is expressed and reinforced in such a way that people want to follow and contribute to it.

Great team leaders are excellent communicators, capable of persuading their teams to reach for higher and higher levels of accomplishment. They are the core, and their vision spreads throughout the entire organization.

Fisher DeBerry is the former head football coach of the U.S. Air Force Academy. During his 22-year career there, he became the winningest coach in service academy history. He was selected to the College Football Hall of Fame in 2011, and is widely considered one of the greatest coaches of his time. During our interview, he said, "Each year we had a motto, and we allowed the kids to choose that motto. They'd make recommendations, and we'd discuss them as a staff, look at each one of them as it related to the team, and then the coaching staff would choose a motto, and we'd saturate them with it—on T-shirts and on placards in the meeting rooms, and every day the coaches would say something to that particular motto as it related to the team and its personality." This is how you build core leadership. You infuse every part of the organization and your employees with your motto and your mission.

The core should also communicate a focus and positivity toward the end result of teamwork and each individual's role in working toward a successful end result. High energy, enthusiasm, and a respect for one another should spread and grow throughout the organization. Don't assume that your authority alone is powerful enough to get all the members of your team on the same page. It's up to you to communicate effectively, if not outright convince your team that you have selected the right path that will lead to success for everyone. If you truly believe this and can convey it at every level, in an enthusiastic and upbeat style that calls for "above and beyond" effort that starts with you and works its way throughout your team, then you will create extraordinary results.

Same Rules, New Game

Today's team building requires, if not demands, valuing the individual. There are just too many alternatives that your talented team members can take if they feel uncared for and forgotten. The old school thought process might be, "Fine, let them leave. They need me more than I need them." But assuming that you've already moved forward with and implemented the procedures that find you the best talent, developed those people to their fullest, placed them in the appropriate positions, and directed them toward your goals, since you've expended all the time, effort, and resources required to do this, why wouldn't you do everything you can to hold on to your most valuable assets—people?

Thus, communicating with a younger generation of employees is vital to creating and retaining success. The things that motivated the productive and determined baby boomers and Gen X are not the same things that push the ultra-driven and highly intelligent workers of Gen Y.

We are all a product of the people, places, and experiences that have crossed our path throughout life's journey. The same holds true for our generational peer group. The world in the 1960s and 1970s was an entirely different place from that created by the dynamic changes that took place throughout the 1980s and 1990s. Each of us looks at life's reality through a different set of "perspective glasses." That shouldn't be an excuse to take away from the core principles that have led to the creation of great teams in the past, but it should be an indicator of the need for adaptability in building great teams in the future.

The concept of team hasn't changed over the decades, but the way you go about coaching and managing a team to success has. The rules may be the same, but the way the game is played is considerably different. So you have to change your execution strategy to coincide with the new conditions. The sooner team leaders realize this, the sooner they'll be on track to achieving the goals and benchmarks that will lead to mission success. Cultivate the individuals and you'll strengthen each and every fiber of your team. It takes more effort, more concentration, more tracking, and more maintenance and management, but your efforts will surely be rewarded by highly productive and loyal team members who are willing to put the needs of the organization ahead of their own because they know you're looking out for them.

If there's only one detail or aspect of this book that you take away to enhance the effectiveness of your own team, it should be this: treat each and every team member as if he's your most important "cog in the machine." That doesn't mean that you have to coddle him, cater to him, or otherwise kow-tow to his every request. What it does mean is that you need to establish a positive work environment that each team member realizes will enhance his opportunities. Build your team by building trust. This means meaning what you say and saying what you mean.

Coach DeBerry said, "We'd tell our team members up front that we believed in them, that they had got something special and something to offer the team, and that they should trust us. We were going to find the right place for each player. We were trying to build 'team before self,' and whatever decision we made for you was in the best interest of the team."

Don't expect to take this new generation through "on-the-job training" to get what you want and need from them. You're first going to have to reach out and teach them what your needs and requirements are. Then, as Bruce Tulgan noted, "Spell out for your Gen Yers exactly what they must do to get your assistance in getting their needs met. Help them help you help them."

For many leaders, it's going to take some time to both incorporate this new mindset into their team's culture and implement it within their team's operational plan. It's a total shift in paradigm from past principles in team building.

Teams at Work 14: The Iditarod Trail Sled Dog Race

An annual long-distance sled dog race . . . from Anchorage to Nome [Alaska]. Mushers and a team of 12–16 dogs cover the distance in 9–15 days. Teams frequently race through blizzards causing whiteout conditions, sub-zero temperatures and gale-force winds which can cause the wind chill to reach −100°F (−73°C). The trail is through a harsh landscape of tundra and spruce forests, over hills and mountain passes, and across rivers. . . . The Iditarod is regarded as a symbolic link to the early history of the state and is connected to many traditions commemorating the legacy of dog mushing. More than 50 mushers enter each year.

As of 2006, [one musher estimated] the combined cost of the entry fee, dog maintenance, and transportation to be $20,000 to $30,000. But that figure varies depending upon how many dogs a musher has, what the musher feeds the dogs and how much is spent on housing and handlers. Expenses faced by modern teams include lightweight gear including thousands of booties and quick-change runners, special high-energy dog foods, veterinary care, and breeding costs.

Each team is composed of twelve to sixteen dogs, and no more may be added during the race. At least six dogs must be in harness when crossing the finish line in Nome. The dogs are well-conditioned athletes. Modern racing dogs are all mixed-breed huskies bred for speed, tough feet, endurance, good attitude, and most importantly the desire to run. Training starts in late summer or early fall and intensifies between November and March; competitive teams run 2,000 miles before the race. When there is no snow, dog drivers train using wheeled carts or all-terrain vehicles set in neutral.

Teamwork is essential to success in this race. From the participants to the dogs to the surrounding community, everyone plays a role. Volunteerism is key to the Iditarod, and indigenous people play a central role. The Athabascan in Nikolai are hunters who place great importance on sharing all resources. The children in Nikolai run a restaurant solely for the Iditarod mushers, and adults are chosen to volunteer by drawing names from a hat. There is one large building in the village that serves as a place to sleep for those mushers who decide to take their 24-hour break here. Other Athabascan villages on the trail include Galena, Nulato, and Kaltag. Without the teamwork and support of the surrounding communities, there would be very little chance that any of these teams would ever cross the finish line. (Based on "Iditarod Trail Sled Dog Race," *Wikipedia*, January 17, 2013.)

Maximize Your Strategy

Up to this point, we have discussed the importance of standardizing your approach to leadership and execution, communicating your message to your organization, and transforming it into the rock-solid core that all good companies need in the middle, not necessarily at the top. The game has changed, and now it is your turn to do the same. Some fine tuning of your strategy can turn the volume up a notch to ensure that all of your employees hear you loud and clear.

To maximize your strategy and optimize your game plan, you have to focus on the following six areas of your company:

The elevators

The technology

The finances

The feedback

The roots

The competition

These six areas are generally where the cracks in the foundation develop that allow the success and character of your company to fall through. If you maintain these six independent but crucial pieces, your company will constantly be rising toward higher pinnacles.

The Elevators

Just as elevators in your company go up and down, traveling to and from different floors, so should information. There is enormous value in creating a positive environment in which every department can review and report on details of its operations. We are all part of the same web, interconnected and reliant upon one another to exist, so the journey of information should reflect this relationship. Michael Evans from Vines of Mendoza said, "We do whatever we can to create clear lines of communication in all directions, so that everyone's input and participation is not only valued, but critical to our success."

In the business world, today's teams are apt to be subdivided into various specialties that relate to and interlock with mission accomplishment. In most corporations, there are teams within the team, many of them having their own unique goals and responsibilities that intertwine with the workings of other departments around the company.

It makes good sense to separate the operations of these subsidiary teams from those of the primary team, as the talent, resources, time constraints, and focus can frequently appear to have counterparts within the company. This creates a bit of a dichotomy of emphasis at times. The great teams are able to apportion their efforts without isolating these specialized tasks from the rest of the group. This is how you come to "the whole is greater than the sum of its parts." Without this notion, big corporations and larger teams truly become a "house divided."

Teams that understand this potential pitfall will create an environment in which there is a free flow of communication between departments, regardless of the logistical difficulties. This starts with a firm awareness of the different departments' operations and how they potentially and ultimately affect the efforts of other areas of the team.

This very dilemma within the U.S. Army's procurement process is what inspired my partner at Eye-Scout, Inc. (Steve Burkett), and me to develop what we call the RACE (Real-Time Analysis Collaborative Environment) solution. The acronym itself describes the power of the tool we've provided to program managers: instant communication and exchange of data across channels between subcontractors and departments that in the past were blocked. To summarize all this military jargon, the different facets of a project can communicate with one another more efficiently, and program managers are capable of overseeing a more integrated "bird's-eye view" of their project.

This type of interactive innovation is what great teams will move toward as the various departments and groups that make up their organization require more and more timely and accurate feedback from one another to coordinate their efforts. These teams will be better suited to face the dynamic environments and situations that look to throw them "off course."

The Technology

The way information is disseminated is just as important as the information itself. Technology has exploded in the past 20 years as a result of advances in the power of microprocessors. When I first started working for the Denver Broncos in 1992, information was a coveted element when it came to influencing decision makers. Widespread use of low-cost computers has transformed not only the business world, but also society in general. As improvements in these little "powerhouse" chips of knowledge accelerated, so did developments in everything from the auto industry to household appliances, industrial processing, and even cellular phones. Really, the only thing that limits us with this tremendous gift of data processing is our own innovative thought.

Those teams that can readily identify the challenges they face in communicating at various levels within the group, then efficiently take advantage of the information technology available to them to improve inner and outward connections will surpass their competitors. Given the technological media that are available to an organization, it is inexcusable that even the largest of companies is not connected with its employees and different teams. Without timely and detailed communication, the direction from various angles within the team will not get through in the manner it should. There's no way your team will achieve its goals without all the "cogs turning in unison."

We've discussed the dynamics that affect an object in motion—in this case, your team's plan for mission accomplishment. These variables move at the speed of light, and your ability to respond in a quick and effective manner can mean the difference between victory and defeat. Advances in communication technology are moving just as fast, so keep in mind the importance of knowing the difference between enhancing your team's performance with technology upgrades and otherwise altering your operations with technology.

Look for tools that improve the real-time flow of information among your team members and give you the greatest capacity for reviewing these lateral communications by providing timely, detailed, and effective feedback as it relates to their ongoing efforts.

The Finances

Most businesses are initially created to turn a profit and create income. As they grow, they find other purposes and meaningful ways to have a positive impact on the world, but it all starts with creating a product or providing a service that people want to pay for. At the center of this is the American dollar. The input and output of cash is imperative to the success of any company. But too many companies are unaware or unbalanced when it comes to their financial health. After they flatline, a simple evaluation of the years leading up to this unfortunate result will generally show that the writing was on the wall.

Transparency is the new buzzword in business and in politics. The need for timely and accurate information is at a premium in our interconnected and intertwined lives.

Whether through profit margins, production costs, or payroll and benefits, much of your team's success will be dependent upon the bottom line. Perhaps no other area of a team's operations is so closely guarded as the accountant's books. Yet so much rides on your own decision making and that of your team's midlevel management when it comes to how you manage your finances. A broader understanding of the team's constraints can go a long way in building internal support and cooperation. Find a way to give your team some ownership in this critical capacity for reaching mission accomplishment.

This tiny piece of ownership can go a long way in creating the environment I spoke of earlier that motivates and inspires team members to find new and more efficient ways of executing their responsibilities and directing them toward mission accomplishment. Think of it like those electronic signs that indicate your speed via built-in radar. Most of the time you don't think about slowing down by five miles per hour, but when you visually see that you're over the speed limit, your foot comes off that accelerator rather quickly. Give your team a vision of the speed limit!

Teams at Work 15: Hartsfield-Jackson Atlanta International Airport, "The Busiest Airport in the World"
The future of Hartsfield-Jackson—and aviation—wasn't always so sure. The Airport began as a racetrack owned by the founder of Coca-Cola. When that business failed, early pilots used the straight areas of the track as landing strips.

In 1912 thousands flocked to the field to see a new kind of race: an airplane (piloted by Lincoln Beachey) vs. a Sterns race car (driven by Thornton Leverett). Neck and neck the two men scrambled around the turns toward the finish line. And the winner was . . . the automobile, by four seconds (taken from Atlanta-airport.com). (From *Hartsfield-Jackson News*, July 2009.)

Hartsfield-Jackson Atlanta International Airport has served the most passengers per year (92 million in 2011) since 1998 and the most takeoffs and landings per year (923,991 in 2011) since 2005. Its international service ranks it seventh, with flights to and from North American, South America, Central America, Europe, Asia, and Africa. Terminal and taxiway expansion will allow the airport to accommodate the world's largest passenger airliner, the Airbus A380.

This immense amount of air traffic requires a highly coordinated control system to oversee some 237 flights in and out per hour. The control tower itself is the tallest in the United States, at over 398 feet, and is used to oversee three areas of emphasis: air control, ground control, and flight data/clearance delivery. Apron control and ground movement functions are also part of the tower's (TWR) responsibility. Safety and efficiency are top priorities, and it takes multiple teams of controllers to operate the system. There are seven terminal and concourse areas for passenger boarding: five dedicated to domestic flight activity, and two dedicated directly to international flights. Hartsfield-Jackson Atlanta's concourses are all connected via an underground transportation mall centered on the "plane train," the world's busiest people mover, with 64 million passengers (2002).

There are concessionaires, a bank, conference and office space, and an interfaith chapel, along with airport operations such as check-in, baggage claim, and Customs and Immigration. Hartsfield-Jackson Atlanta employs approximately 55,300 airline, ground transportation, concessionaire, security, federal, state, and city of Atlanta employees. It is the largest employment center in the state of Georgia, with an economic impact of $3.2 billion.

But the numbers are even more daunting. Consider how much teamwork goes into an airport that averages 230,000 passengers each day, 1,224 daily domestic departures, 178 U.S. destinations with nonstop service from Atlanta, 741 weekly nonstop international departures, 80 international destinations with nonstop service from Atlanta, 2,700 arrivals/departures daily, 136,506 domestic seats available daily, more than 108,845 international seats available weekly, and 33 passenger airlines served.

The Feedback

The last of the "big four" elements involved in the strategic execution of your game plan is the manner in which you receive feedback from your employees and customers. Author Ken Blanchard said, "Feedback is the breakfast of champions." It is crucial that you build a system that allows for multiple inputs from all angles of the organization, both internally and externally.

A common thread that seems to flow through everything we've discussed is the internal need for real communication among team members at every level. Find me a failure in the history of team building, and ultimately I'll bet you that it circles back to this singular inherent flaw in most organizations.

Providing a conduit for discussion and input gives your team true operational ownership of its actions. It provides leaders with internal feedback. Team members then become an active part of the solution to problems that get in the way of focus, unity, direction, and excellence.

Many workers are diverse in their own understanding and talents with regard to your mission. Your own versions of the council can open doors for input from every angle. But make sure this is done in a positive manner. Dana Perino told me, "As a blessed American, I steer away from negativity. If I ever feel myself descending into a rant about something, I try to remind myself that any problem I'm facing is nothing compared with the challenges that 90 percent of the world deals with daily. I try to be positive whenever possible, because if I'm down, they will be down. And if the team leader isn't projecting a positive outlook, you can devolve quickly. The boss will expect bad news and problems to come up, but showing a sunny side helps keep the wheels turning in a positive direction."

But it does not stop there. Feedback should not be limited to internal responses. External information and knowledge from the consumer are undeniably helpful in the growth of your business. If you know what your consumers want, you can provide them with what they need. Any business can find value and appeal in a basic understanding of the general public's opinion. This can be accomplished through polling, hosting free public events, direct mailers and e-mails, phone calls, and even speaking with your customers directly. The feedback you receive should come from many different directions and angles, but with the goal of recognizing and appreciating what the essential feedback of your employees and customers will offer.

The Roots

After you have reviewed the nuts and bolts of your business, it is time to look at the origins of it. Embracing past accomplishments to emphasize team development is a powerful way to create inspired and motivated employees. Great companies have left legacies of success. Political leader Marcus Garvey said, "A people without the knowledge of their past history, origin and culture is like a tree without roots." The pride and prestige of past accomplishments have inspired succeeding generations of team members to carry on that heritage. Given the opportunity, people want to be identified with and part of a winning team. Being associated with successful teams somehow allows us to embody the positive aspects of their culture in our own character.

By embracing the past, you're displaying a respect for your organization's foundation, the people and particulars that got you to this point in time. Perhaps there were great sacrifices made by former employees, tremendous challenges overcome, and achievements that had never before been reached until those employees actually did so. These all work to spark your workforce and stimulate a culture of excellence based on what was and what can be. Coach DeBerry said, "Coaching the Air Force Academy was as much about our past as it was about our future. We were all proud to represent an institution that had a purpose, and that purpose was built into the core values of integrity above all, and you have to love one another if you're going to have that integrity—service before self. That's when the team becomes much bigger than you. It's amazing what you can accomplish when nobody cares who gets the credit, a concept instilled throughout the Air Force Academy's rich history."

Platforms for communication and feedback with current employees can give the pioneers of your organization a conduit for passing on this "legacy of excellence." Establishing the mentorship programs discussed earlier and considering the courage to allow "old coaches" to have a chance to interact with team members can be a healthy way in which to emphasize the history of your organization. Successful organizations that draw upon previous success, but don't dwell upon it, can use this positive energy to ignite their current efforts toward the attainment of future goals.

Don't be afraid of your organization's past. A team that knows where it's been knows where it's going. Although the ever-changing present dynamics that make the past appear irrelevant often lead to its being dismissed, there's still plenty to be learned from those who paved the way for the current opportunities and success that your employees might be enjoying today. Weave these threads of experience into the fabric of your business and you'll be stronger as a result.

The Competition

Up to this point, we have looked internally. However, understanding your external competition and how other organizations not only succeed, but also fail, can offer valuable insight and pointers. Passionate individuals tend to pour themselves deeply into their work. Walt Disney said, "I have been up against tough competition all my life. I wouldn't know how to get along without it." Leaders are expected to be the experts in their particular industry. Given the availability of research and related publications, the great team leaders seek out opportunities to study their respective industries and embrace the competition. They analyze statistical data and varying trends in their own marketplace.

Throughout my tenure as general manager of the Broncos, I regularly studied where we fit in various categories that related to the business of putting together a professional football team. We were able to develop numerous reports that clarified our own efforts relative to league averages. But we took things one step further: we broke down these data to compare them with each of the other 31 clubs. At any point in time, I had the ability to answer questions and report back to the owners not only on how the Broncos stood against the league as a whole, but also on how we were operating head to head with our own divisional rivals and the rest of the competition.

The idea wasn't necessarily to highlight our strengths or weaknesses relative to others, but to identify those teams that we felt were doing things in an efficient manner and to learn from their success. This was one of our most anticipated reports at the end of every season, and one that helped guide our thoughts as we worked to improve for the following year.

The information was always presented in a clear, concise, and easy-to-understand manual. A lot of the data were provided visually through graphs and charts. Too often, in attempting to explain things as thoroughly as possible, teams lose sight of the ultimate purpose of studies, analysis, and reports— communicative feedback. The goal is to enhance your own self-evaluation, not to confuse the issue. By providing this feedback in a manner that is easy to comprehend, you're giving your employees the necessary intelligence to adjust their efforts and stay the course. Life isn't lived in a vacuum, nor is business conducted in one.

Coach DeBerry told me, "I think you do have to know your competitors, and you do have to know what makes them tick so that you can counter what they do. Leading is about understanding the market and the role you play within it."

A firm grasp on the handle of your industry can provide your employees with the context they need in developing, analyzing, and executing your operational plan. You'll have the necessary flexibility to adjust on the fly and the knowledge you need to place resources where they're needed most. More important, you'll display the leadership necessary to get your organization to follow you through tough times, knowing full well that your actions are based upon grounded principles as they relate to the dynamics of your industry.

Sun Tzu said, "All men can see these tactics whereby I conquer, but what none can see is the strategy out of which victory is evolved." This chapter should give you all you need if you are to understand the manufacturing of success. We have all seen great ends: Apple, Facebook, Walmart, Google, Microsoft, and numerous other "role-model" companies. The strategy behind these companies is what built them into the financial juggernauts they are today. The execution and optimization of the Xs and the Os is truly where the rubber meets the road. By focusing your time and attention on communicating, leadership, and the internal and external forces and parts that push and pull upon your business, you can begin to make the necessary adjustments and enhancements to harvest a fruitful and bountiful organization.

CHAPTER 6

THE FAILURES: DEALING WITH ADVERSITY

T
eams work hard to reach a common goal, but sometimes they fall short. When they do, the way the leader responds can make all the difference in the company's future. This chapter focuses on how a leader should respond when obstacles arise and misfortune strikes. Whether the issue is challenges from the inside (which are controllable) or from the outside (which often are not), maintaining team morale and reaching goals are imperative for the overall triumph of an organization. Too often, bad times breed bad habits, which can result in enormous fallout, even after the problem is solved.

This chapter gives the reader everything you need to know if you are to manage adversity and turn negatives into positives. In the NFL, just as in business, there are extreme highs and extreme lows. Misfortune has no conscience, and it can strike at the most unexpected moments. Thus, the best leaders and organizations have systematic plans in place to deal with difficult experiences. This chapter will give leaders the know-how to avoid problematic situations, maintain team composure when such situations do occur, and rebound from challenges, coming out even stronger than before.

For years ABC's *Wide World of Sports* opened its program with host Jim McKay's iconic catchphrase, "The thrill of victory and the agony of defeat." To further dramatize the program's introduction, a short clip of Yugoslavian ski jumper Vinko Bogataj's horrific fall at the 1970 World Championships was played. Bogataj miscalculated his adjustment to changing conditions on the ramp and flew uncontrollably into a nearby retaining fence. He miraculously escaped serious injury (if not death) and actually returned to compete the following season. However, this moment of adversity lived in infamy.

The very nature of sports (and business) forces team members to face various levels of adversity and even outright loss. The core of athletic competition involves participants' ability to rise, fall, and then rise again in the face of this adversity. This is why sports are such tremendous metaphors for life and for business: both involve facing loss and hardship.

Perhaps the late Israeli prime minister Golda Meir put it best when she said, "You'll never find a better sparring partner than adversity." Adversity is going to find a way to attack your team's efforts from every angle. All teams will face internal trials and tribulations that can damage their ability to accomplish the mission and achieve their goals. Most of these come in the form of strains on the structural and procedural aspects of your short- and long-term endeavors.

Ed Roski told me,

Adversity occurs—it's as simple as that. You find road-blocks, barriers, and closed doors. The goal is to find a way around them, over them, under them, or through them. It is vital that your team understands that there will be some good things and some challenging ones during the course of any project. You just have to figure out the situation and get excited when people come up with alternatives to achieve the goals. It is about bringing everyone together, understanding the challenge, and how you're going to overcome it. Sometimes it is just about getting everyone in the boat and rowing together through the waves of adversity.

We've discussed the critical importance of finding the best and the brightest team members, and no doubt you've put a lot of energy and resources into doing so, while simultaneously developing a dependence on and connection to their efforts and production. But inevitably your team will be faced with the need to replace high-level leaders and strong midlevel managers, as well as some of your most productive and skilled team members at various levels of operations. Losing one or more cogs can easily bring your team to an abrupt halt.

Adversity is the great unknown, but how you handle it is not. Having a game plan for adversity is vital to how quickly you rebound from it. Valuable time, money, and resources are often wasted on the rebound process. But they do not have to be. Studying your market, evaluating where the pitfalls may be, and implementing a systematic and quick response system can turn a negative scenario into a positive one.

The Internal and External Struggle

In business, adversity will present itself in one of two forms: internal or external. Internal adversity can appear in the form of issues with management, employee competition, team unhappiness, a loss of focus on the overall mission and goals, and falling short of internal expectations. Internal dissension and conflict can revolve around personnel, as even the best of teams must deal head-on with the human element. Discourse among leaders and team members, between teammates, and even at the management level can create a crippling "ripple effect" within the ranks — top down, bottom up, and inside out.

Internal logistical problems can bog down your efforts and produce tipping points in your timeline of operations. Time constraints, financial restrictions, communication lapses, and the ineffective allocation of any other essential resources needed by your team can hinder even the best-focused intentions and quickly lead to major trouble.

But you don't have the inner challenges that can either slowly chip away or intensely hack at your team's unity. Yours is a well-oiled machine, working in singular harmony across all spectrums of internal operations. Your plans are well constructed, your team members are supportive of one another's efforts, and your leadership is working to maximize efficiency.

Frequently, internal problems develop as a result of external results and pressure. The external adversity squeezes the company so strongly that even the most protected and best shielded team members begin to feel the strain. This is where true team building is revealed. Teams that succumb to the negative stress of dissension, bickering, and conflict were never really teams at all. Real teams maintain their focus, unity, direction, and excellence in the face of all forms of adversity. As famed author Arthur Golden put it, "Adversity is like a strong wind. It tears away from us all but the things that cannot be torn, so that we see ourselves as we really are."

Is your team strong enough to withstand erosion in confidence or the development of complacency as a result of a lack of success? Can your team resist splintering into cliques, playing the "blame game," or the creation of conflicting agendas? Adversity can disrupt your coordinated efforts, despite your best-laid plans. Teams that crack under external pressures and that don't remain focused on the mission, understand the context, and remain committed to one another will begin to try to protect individual interests and maintain the status quo.

Teams with well-developed internal strength can withstand the strong winds of adversity. They see temporary setbacks as opportunities for growth. Much like a broken bone, they heal at the point of fracture and will end up even stronger than before. These teams bond through a shared commitment to the overall mission. Individuals put the needs of the team and their teammates ahead of their own. A collective determination to overcome can energize an entire organization, despite whatever setbacks it might be facing.

Much of the external strain comes from the competition. More than ever, consumers have endless options and opportunities for spending their hard-earned money. If you were the only shark in the sea, it would be easy to find dinner. However, the nature of our market dictates that unless you evolve, compete, and work hard for your business, you will shrivel up and disappear. You are always in competition with the team that won the big contract, captured its third straight quarter over you, or won the game by 27 points.

How did you respond to an increase in the price of widgets? Or what about new government regulation that puts a damper on your production process? Were you prepared for the influx of technological advances that have now made your product irrelevant and obsolete? Most of the external forces working against you are dynamic in nature: sudden changes in the industry; superior strength in your opponents; unforeseen circumstances in intrabusiness operations. What's even more disconcerting is the fact that external adversity can multiply internal weaknesses in your team.

Teams at Work 16: Hoover Dam, aka Boulder Dam

[The Hoover Dam's] construction was the result of a massive effort involving thousands of workers, and cost over one hundred lives. . . .

In 1928, Congress authorized the project. The winning bid to build the dam was submitted by a consortium called Six Companies, Inc., which began construction on the dam in early 1931. Such a large concrete structure had never been built before, and some of the techniques were unproven. The torrid summer weather and the lack of facilities near the site also presented difficulties. Nevertheless, Six Companies turned over the dam to the federal government on March 1, 1936.

Once construction began, Six Companies hired large numbers of workers, with more than 3,000 on the payroll by 1932 and employment peaking at 5,251 in July 1934.

In sheer numbers, the dam is 726.4 feet high, 1,244 feet across at the top, 660 feet thick at the base, and 45 feet thick at the top. It weighs 6.6 million tons, can store up to two years' "average" flow from the Colorado River, and has a total storage capacity of 30,500,000 acre-feet. Building such an imposing structure in 1930 could be accomplished only through one thing: teamwork. The technology was far from standard, and some declared that the structure was impossible to build. However, through the dedication and planning of one rock-solid team, it was completed nearly two years ahead of schedule. (Based on "Hoover Dam," *Wikipedia*, January 23, 2013.)

Adversity will find its way into the cracks and crevices of your business. If there are any weaknesses, they will be exposed. In business, you cannot operate by hoping that adversity will never occur. Wouldn't it be nice if things were that easy? Team leaders could just sit back and rely on the inherent strength of individuals to press on toward the common goal.

There would be no need to worry about any negative effects of hardship, misfortune, or loss. There would be no such thing as losing streaks or downtrends. Teams that were hit with adversity would just switch to autopilot and self-correct to deal with forces that were trying to knock them off the path.

Unfortunately, that is not the way things are likely to happen. It is not a matter of *if* adversity will occur, but rather *when* and *at what capacity*. Sometimes adversity is small and easily manageable. Other times, it is enormous and has catastrophic results. Alan Lakein said, "Failing to plan is planning to fail." Adversity can and should be planned for. It should be studied, evaluated, and prepared for. Any top-notch business leader sculpts his adversity response system as the culmination of the business plan. If you have not done so, you should do it now. Adversity is swimming down the stream of success. Where, when, and how hard it hits are unpredictable, but its occurrence is inevitable.

The Silver Lining of Adversity

While there's no such thing as a self-correcting autopilot in team building, you can take the necessary steps to transform adversity into positive lessons for renewed growth in your team. You must begin by communicating the context and understanding how a setback has affected your overall efforts in order to make the necessary corrections and right the course. If you can quickly pinpoint the dynamic factors that led to the adversity, you can determine the proper path to take to ensure that it doesn't happen again. And really that's the point: building strength where there once was weakness.

Great teams seize this opportunity through self-evaluation and corresponding adjustments. Team members are made aware of the problem, told of its causes, shown the context of its ramifications, and then presented with the direction to be taken to overcome the adversity. Teams that have strong, confident leadership will seek internal feedback from team members concerning the causes and be open to the possibility of internally generated solutions. The ability to listen and give your team a conduit for communication in times of stress creates an even stronger, broader-based sense of ownership in mission accomplishment.

Shane Richardson is the chief executive officer of the South Sydney Rabbitohs, the most successful rugby team in the history of the Australian Rugby League. He has been with the team since 2004 and is the longest-serving CEO in the game. In our interview, he stressed the importance of communication by telling me, "The greater the obstacle, the more we focus on communication: breaking down the problem and dealing with it as a group, rather than as individuals; encouraging people to put their hands up early to get assistance. 'You' don't have a problem, 'we' do. When it comes to adversity, we tell our entire club to reset goals, refocus, and ask what they can do better."

Don't be so quick to have all the answers and solutions, even if you do.

When lines of communication are open and flowing, your team members gain confidence in their level of importance for mission accomplishment. When problems are analyzed and quickly corrected, team members are assured that the leaders care about the operational aspects of the mission and team members' role in it.

When teams don't use the close eye of evaluation, but rather focus solely on the loss or setback and then procrastinate in seeking solutions, there is sure to be trouble. Finger-pointing begins, apathy appears, and an erosion of faith in the leaders is sure to occur. If team members don't know the direction to take and the steps to carry out, they will create their own individual agendas.

To put it in a simpler perspective, imagine a multistranded wire or cable that carries electricity from point A to point B. When it is tightly bound and securely insulated, the wire has stronger conductivity and a greater ability to carry a current more efficiently. But when the wire is laid open and frayed at any point along its length, it loses the strength that inherently comes from a solid bundle. Conductivity is diminished, and the wire becomes more susceptible to fatigue and breakage at the point where it is frayed.

Miles and miles of efficient current flow can suddenly cease as a result of the smallest of fractures. What remains intact isn't capable of carrying the same load that was originally intended. Frayed strands can short-circuit and ignite a fire. Again, it's no coincidence that your ability to fight off and cope with adversity goes back to the very beginning: selecting team members with excellent character and a strong commitment.

When I was general manager of the Denver Broncos, we knew that there was going to be adversity throughout the season. The best teams in the NFL are those that can handle the inevitable struggles of a 17-week season and enter the playoffs stronger as a result. Injuries, team attitude, competitors' behavior, and the media can all fray your wire and cause discontent within the organization. Something as small as a missed tackle or a dropped pass, or as big as a season-ending knee injury or a three-game losing streak, can have an effect (short and long term) on the performance of your roster.

Understanding and accepting the value of the silver lining found in adversity will help to motivate you to change your attitude and your team to view the obstacles as meaningful experiences. Maya Angelou said, "If you don't like something, change it. If you can't change it, change your attitude." Your perception of adversity is just as important as the actual challenge itself. Your attitude toward adversity will be felt throughout the entire organization, and team members are likely to take a similar approach. If your team shuts down in the face of adversity, this is probably a reflection of the example you have created. The ability to plan and manage adversity is in your hands, and if you focus on the silver lining that comes with it, you will find that coping with it is easier than you originally forecasted.

The Pitfalls of Adversity

We have established that adversity occurs both internally and externally and that it comes with a silver lining that, if focused upon, can propel your team to change the negatives into positives. However, adversity has its pitfalls as well. No matter how much you plan for it or how well you handle it when it appears, it can still have a negative impact on your organization.

The Irish writer and poet Oscar Wilde once said, "Experience is the name so many people give to their mistakes." Most general managers of NFL football teams would prefer working with both talented and experienced players. Veterans are savvy concerning the varieties of adversity that can take their toll on a team's efforts. Experienced players know the importance of preparation, work ethic, and continuing high-level performance. They've seen the value of teammates stepping up to fill in for injured stars, perhaps having been called upon to do so themselves in the past. They've shown the necessary flexibility in adjusting their game plans and aren't easily rattled by setbacks. In other words, they've made their mistakes.

Understandably, rookies are less likely to be prepared for adversity. They fail to understand the importance of putting struggles in their proper perspective—an understanding that can come only through having previously struggled and persevered. Wouldn't it be great if your team were full of Pro Bowl veteran players—a team loaded with depth and experience that was able to withstand any game lapse, devastating injury, or string of multiple losses? You'd hoist your own version of the Lombardi Trophy many times if that were the case.

But in both football and business, the reality is that there's a finite set of highly skilled and extremely experienced "players" out there, not to mention limits on employing them that result from financial constraints. You're going to have personnel who can't handle the stress and don't respond to pressure well, and you'd better know which wires are more likely to fray when they're put under a heavy load.

Train for Adversity

The best way to ensure that both the leaders and the team members have the confidence to overcome any problems you might face is to plan and train for those problems before they happen. You're well served if you are aware of and fully understand the potential pitfalls that can hit you at any time and from any angle. My military career as an intelligence officer in Berlin, Germany, during the Cold War was all about training and preparation. Critical situations and scenarios were practiced over and over. Most of us had never been to war, but the Air Force ensured that if a war did commence, we'd know what to do and when and how to do it.

Young service members were put through rigorous training exercises to prepare them for facing the unknown, and we all understood that the uncertain future would most likely include taking on and overcoming adversities. As a first lieutenant evaluating my flight of young analysts, I found these types of exercises to be the best and most thorough way to determine who was up to the task and who might need additional work. They readily identified any weaknesses in our operational systems and put our leadership and decision making to the test.

It wasn't any different in the National Football League, as hours and hours of practice in breaking down the game into various subcomponents of emphasis gave the coaches an idea of which players they could count on in the clutch and which would succumb to the pressure of a "must have" performance.

Training exercises will give you a firm awareness of the effect that individuals have on the plans and procedures necessary for achieving your own goals as a team. You'll build a better understanding of the performance levels and production required from every operational level, and the resulting ripple effects on other areas when these levels are not met.

The importance of a good training exercise program for combating the effects of adversity on your team is threefold. First, it develops maximum efficiency, reinforcing high standards of expectation at every level. Second, it gives the leaders a better understanding of where breakdowns might occur so as not to cause a "knee-jerk" reaction with potential fixes or adjustments when they do. And third, it allows you to exercise your team's skill at ensuring that your personnel are positioned with the right fit instead of having to learn such a fit in a time of crisis.

Jeff Pash, general counsel for the NFL, said, "You have to train for adversity. First, you have to make sure everyone understands the feasibility of an outcome and is aware it could happen. Second, you have to train your team to understand what to do if that outcome does occur, to prevent panic and minimize stress on the team. Finally, if you get bad news, don't hide under your desk, because that compounds the problem. Look the issue in the eye and begin to aggressively implement your plan to push through."

As young cadets at the Air Force Academy, we were all required to navigate the Leadership Reaction Course, or LRC. The LRC was a twist on the *MacGyver* TV series, in which teams and their leaders were faced with various obstacle-course-type scenarios designed to constrain their resources, time, and personnel.

Each cadet was given the opportunity to lead her team and devise a plan to move through, over, and around various physical barriers. You might have a ten-foot rope, two six-foot poles, and three duffle bags that you could use to climb over an eight-foot wall, cross a twelve-foot stream, and then maneuver through a simulated minefield. Oh, and you would also have one team member who was unable to walk, but who couldn't be left behind, and 30 minutes to construct and execute your plan. Go!

Those who were successful at the exercise remained calm, took inventory of their strengths, sought out input from team members, and were decisive in their own judgment of how to come out on the other side successfully. Their communication was clear and distinct; everyone knew his role in the solution and worked to accomplish it.

Those who failed panicked under the pressure. They devised a solution on their own, and they took input and rebuttal as they constructed their way out of the problem. Communication was usually through shouting and was negative in construct and tone. They let intermittent hurdles get in the way of the overall goal. In a sense, their team was working as a group of uncoordinated and off-track individuals.

But every cadet who failed in her attempt to complete the LRC came out better for it. The instructional staff reviewed the entire exercise, from initial planning, through midlevel snags, to final solutions, with each team. Everyone learned not only from the leader's mismanaged mistakes, but also from their own as contributing team members.

The value of similar testing for your team is to condition a leadership response when adversity hits and, perhaps, fend it off before it does. Much of dealing with adversity as a leader involves the ability to avoid it altogether, or at least to minimize its effect on your team when it does occur. When you take the time to train your team for the various trials and tribulations it may face, you will already have a group of seasoned veterans before they ever take to the field.

Most teams aren't put under the restrictive limitations that the LRC placed on Air Force Academy cadets. If you've diligently prepared, you will rarely find yourself in a situation or scenario that you haven't planned for in the past. Under adverse conditions, most teams are forced to revise their already existing operations and procedures. They confront their problems confidently with their previously well-planned solutions. Everyone knows his role and responsibility as the group collectively delves into the problem. Suddenly efforts come to a grinding halt—the result of an unforeseen error that is outside of your control.

Here's where your previous training exercises kick in. Your team's leaders know its strengths and turn to the team members to make the necessary adjustments to your plan and bypass the effects of the error on your operations. You're back online.

That's pretty painless. Though the error that brought you down was unforeseen, it wasn't unanticipated. Careful consideration of all the obstacles that could get in your way was inserted into an LRC-style training exercise, and your team's operational plan was put to the test. Some things helped you through, while others were an impediment.

A careful analysis of all operating systems was made, resources were inventoried, equipment was tested, personnel were evaluated, and regulation books were revised. In the end, your team took the time to review the statistics, collect the data, and seek internal feedback. The leaders identified where procedures broke down and tweaked those procedures as a result of team member input. Everyone knew that although the chances that this particular error would occur were slim, the team would be ready to adjust if and when it did occur.

This may seem like high-maintenance management, and to a degree it is. But that's the job of a great team leader: to constantly find ways to maximize your team's individual and overall performance. Your team members are looking to and depending on your direction to reach their goals. You don't have to be an expert in all areas of operations, but you had better know what's required and expected of your team if the job is to get done. If you don't, you won't even know what to look for, and you will find yourself blindly stabbing at solutions or searching for hidden answers as to why your team can't perform under adversity.

Teams at Work 17: Hurricane Katrina

Hurricane Katrina was the second strongest hurricane ever recorded in the U.S.

In New Orleans, the levees were designed for category 3, but Katrina was forecasted in Category 4, [with winds up to a] whopping 140 miles an hour.

The storm surge from Katrina was 20 feet (6 meters) high, [causing more than 1,800 deaths and] 705 people still reported missing as a result.

Hurricane Katrina affected more than 15 million people in different factors such as [through the] economy, evacuations, gas prices or drinking water.

An estimated 80% of New Orleans was under water, up to 20 feet deep in places.

Hurricane Katrina caused $75 billion in estimated physical damages, but it is estimated that the total economic impact in Louisiana and Mississippi may [have exceeded] $110 billion, earning the title of costliest hurricane ever in US history.

Hurricane Katrina affected about 90,000 square miles.

The region supported approximately one million nonfarm jobs, but hundreds of thousands of local residents were left unemployed by the hurricane.

But the real story of Hurricane Katrina comes in its aftermath.

More than 70 countries pledged monetary donations or other assistance. Kuwait made the largest single pledge of $500 million, but Qatar, India, China, Pakistan, and Bangladesh made very large donations as well.

After Katrina, the soul of New Orleans was demolished, but its heart still beat strongly. Today, it has returned to its pre-Katrina form, with businesses and residents returning and prospering once again. But this was made possible only by the team of millions who sent valuable resources and volunteers to help rebuild this beautiful city. (From "11 Facts About Hurricane Katrina," dosomething.org.)

Dealing with Adversity: Analyze, Adjust, and Eliminate

As Jeffrey Benjamin stated, "Unless you have the courage to analyze your mistakes, you are bound to repeat them." Dealing with adversity is just as important as planning for it.

Because you cannot plan for everything, when you are managing adversity, it is imperative that you have a response system in place. It is how you analyze and adjust that will determine your team's ability to overcome in the future. The key to this process is treating both success and failure in a similar manner, with the overall understanding of how each influences the ability to accomplish the mission. If you can achieve this balance, making the necessary revisions in people and procedures becomes a normal and accepted part of your team's culture.

When you are faced with adversity, use this three-tiered approach:

Analyze. Focus on standard planning processes, ensuring constant and consistent communication down through the various levels of your team without panic. It's crucial that your team members understand the need for these processes, and how they will work to positively affect the forces and/or dynamics that caused the struggles in the first place.

Adjust. Move forward with revisions to plans, procedures, and personnel as quickly as possible. Don't let your team get bogged down in red tape and review. If you've practiced your due diligence in all areas of your initial efforts toward building your team, then the subtle tweaks or necessary major changes will be visibly evident. Strong, confident, and effective action is what your team is looking for. Without it, poor performance becomes customary and is more difficult to break free from.

Eliminate. Answers should be provided promptly and with direction. Delay can very easily be interpreted as apathy and indifference. If you don't provide answers promptly, your team members will find their own, and you can only hope that those answers point in the direction of your collective goals. You have to respond to adversity and communicate your desired outcome and strategy. By eliminating the issue, you can get back on track and minimize the damage that potential pitfalls and adversity produce.

The adage "forged under fire" is sometimes used to describe the growth process that takes place when individuals are placed under great stress and strain and emerge wiser and stronger as a result of the experience. Think about it: military officers, emergency room doctors, first responders . . . the list goes on and on. Teams are willing to respond to leaders who are calm and capable of making the right decisions when faced with extreme circumstances.

Teams at Work 18: The Great Pyramid of Giza

The oldest and largest of the three pyramids in the Giza Necropolis. . . . [It is thought to have been] built as a tomb for . . . Egyptian Pharaoh Khufu over a 10 to 20-year period. . . . [It] was the tallest man-made structure in the world for over 3,800 years.

It was one of the Seven Wonders of the Ancient World.

It's estimated to be constructed of 2.3 million blocks, more than 12 of which were moved] into place each hour, day and night, [for twenty years]. . . .

Many disagree on whether the blocks were dragged, lifted, or even rolled into place. [Some believe] that slave labor was used, but modern discoveries . . . suggest it was built instead by tens of thousands of skilled workers . . . consisting of two *gangs* of 100,000 men, divided into five *zaa* or *phyle* of 20,000 men each, which may have been further divided according to the skills of the workers. . . .

A . . . construction management study and . . . Egyptologists, estimate that the total project required an average workforce of 14,567 people and a peak workforce of 40,000. Without the use of pulleys, wheels, or iron tools, they . . . suggest the Great Pyramid was completed from start to finish in approximately 10 years.

The total mass of the Great Pyramid of Giza is estimated to be 5.9 million tons, and its volume is said to be roughly 2,500,000 cubic meters. Consider 100,000 team members (probably one of the biggest teams in history) laying more than 5 million pounds of stone blocks to build these mind-blowing structures. The insurmountable project that these team members undertook, the adversity that they overcame, and the sweat that they shed to complete this project can only make this project go down in history as one of the greatest accomplishments of any team. (Based on "Great Pyramid of Giza," *Wikipedia*, January 23, 2013.)

Beating Adversity

The very essence of "teamwork" revolves around the combination of efforts to produce a result that would be unattainable by an individual. The greater the challenge, the greater the need for well-coordinated and sustainable efforts. With challenge comes adversity, so it's only natural that teams that are brought together in order to face and conquer a challenge will also be required to overcome adversity.

In my interview with Jon Semcken, he said, "You have to let adversity go and not dwell on it. To keep the same team goal, you should consider your temperament and focus. Make change slow: hire slow and fire slow. This will reduce your adversity and allow you to manage your business. You cannot let your team go sideways."

To prevent your team from getting off course, Dana Perino told me, you simply have to focus. "Focus, focus, focus," she said.

There was a time when a book was written about President Bush that I thought was inconsiderate and took way too many cheap shots. I was angry. I couldn't even sleep for thinking of it all night long for three nights. I was snapping at everyone. The president heard I was having trouble getting that one behind me, and he called me into his office and gently asked me to try to forgive the author. I asked, "Can I throw him under the bus first?" He smiled and said, "No." He didn't want me to feel bitter, so when I turned to leave the Oval Office, President Bush showed what I thought was amazing leadership. He said, "By the way, I don't think you'd ever do this to me." He knew exactly what was bothering me—without my even saying it. I went to my office with a whole new attitude, and I barely gave that author another thought.

Think back to the analogy of the wolf pack in nature. Not every hunt will be a successful one, and yet every hunt teaches the pack its strengths and its weaknesses. If the pack isn't able to adapt and learn from a missed kill, it will starve and die. How will your team react to its own challenges and adversity?

Concentrate on bringing together the "Four Rs": recognize, review, revise, and refocus. Nobody likes to lose; the key is just not to make it a bad habit. Staying on the right track with the Four Rs will ensure that your team comes out stronger than before and "forged by fire."

Recognize, It's important to realize that there are problems and adversity in the first place. You must be open-minded regarding the internal and external signs that point directly to the factors that stress your team.

Review. Great teams will have built-in processes that analyze their efforts and give meaningful feedback. These processes help to identify the possible reasons where, how, and why your team faltered under pressure.

Revise. When problems have been acknowledged and the reasons for them identified, teams can begin to revise their efforts wisely through written plans, improved training, new operational procedures, or obtaining new personnel.

Refocus. If your team dwells on adversity and defeat, this will pull at the other areas of unity, direction, and excellence. Refocus your team on accomplishing your mission so that it is once again back on the path to success.

It is important to realize that there will be challenges, there will be obstacles, and you will lose from time to time. That's all just part of being in the game. It's your team's preparation and immediate response that will determine its ability to persevere.

You can't fully avoid adversity if you're going to take on the big challenges in your particular area of interest or industry. However, there are some steps that you can take to lessen the impact of adversity prior to and after its occurrence.

Much of what we've already discussed in building a strong team will help you do just this:

o   Secure the best and most talented team members.

o   Define a clear-cut mission and keep your team unwaveringly focused on the prize.

o   Develop detailed and well-thought-out training programs to maximize performance.

o   Evaluate capabilities, skill, and production to place team members in the right roles.

o   Build and maintain solid procedural plans that lead directly to benchmarked goals and mission accomplishment.

These steps create an inner strength within teams that can sometimes act as a shield against certain forms of adversity. Teams that are built on a strong foundation find ways to

avoid struggles on their own. Members act in the best interest of achieving the mission and see problems before they are
manifested. When sound procedures are in place, teams can
act quickly to rectify situations that might otherwise result in a
losing scenario. It's somewhat like a homeopathic healing process or, better yet, preventive medicine for your team's health.

These suggestions will help you fight against internal
struggles and parry some external ones, but there will be some
body blows that you will need to deal with. For these, your
team will be best served by well-conceived "emergency" training and action plans. Test your team and create confidence
through training exercises, ongoing individual development,
and continued evaluative analysis and feedback.

The 1972 Miami Dolphins are the only team in the history
of the NFL to go undefeated to win a Super Bowl championship. That means that thousands of times, even the best teams
in the world have lost. The best of the best in professional football are going to fall at some point during the season. It's how
they respond to the questions and criticism from pundits and
elsewhere that builds championship-caliber organizations. It's
how the players come back and practice the following week.
It's how the coaching staff adjusts the game plan to handle an
upcoming opponent. It's the ability of the organization to realize that this is only a setback. These are the teams that quickly
turn a single loss into a five- or six-game winning streak.

Michael Evans of Vines of Mendoza told me that beating
adversity comes down to three things: "Number one, building an amazing team; number two, working extremely hard to
plan and strategize; and, number three, never giving up." No
matter what industry you are a part of, adversity will be a factor

in the development or the deterioration of your business. You are going to have to pay the price that comes with it, and, based on years of watching successful teams succumb to its will, I can tell you that the up-front amount will be much less expensive than if you finance it over time. Prepare for adversity early, so that you don't have to pay for it later. William Arthur Ward said, "Adversity causes some men to break, others to break records." We all want to be part of the elite, yet small, group of record-breaking companies. But to do so, you have to invest the time and effort into your company, your strategy, and your team.

CHAPTER 7

SUCCESS: MAINTAINING EXCELLENCE THROUGH TEAMWORK

Y ou've made it this far. You've hired great talent, created a rock-solid mission statement, implemented a strong game plan, and dealt with adversity along the way. But one question lingers: how do I, as a leader, push forward, reach higher, and handle all of the success my company has seen? To be honest, staying on top is just as hard as getting there to begin with. The good news is that there are tried and true ways to maintain excellence and infuse your team with an understanding of how to handle success at the highest levels.

Aristotle said, "Excellence is an art won by training and habituation. We do not act rightly because we have virtue or excellence, but we rather have those because we have acted rightly. We are what we repeatedly do. Excellence, then, is not an act but a habit." This chapter will give you everything you need to know in order to manage a great team's triumphs and form the habit of excellence.

In my interview with renowned sports agent Molly Fletcher, she said,

Maintaining excellence calls for two very simple but often lost characteristics: discipline and execution. Professional athletes, national championship head coaches, world championship head coaches, and Emmy award–winning broadcasters are on the stage that they are on because of their discipline and their ability to execute — execute in the bottom of the ninth inning or on the free throw line with two seconds left — and to have the knowledge and the guts to make the right call on 4th and 4 to win the game. The ability to deliver in key moments consistently is what separates the best from the rest.

From understanding what victory does to a team's mentality to maintaining happy team members to preserving an environment of accomplishment, this chapter offers readers insight into what makes a successful team remain motivated, inspired, and positive while preventing complacency and a "glass ceiling" mentality as its members reach their goals and attain their objectives. There is no doubt that success can corrupt even the tightest-knit teams if it is not handled properly by leaders and upper management. Excellence should be welcomed and celebrated, but the need to sustain that excellence should be expected and anticipated. This chapter will push you to understand the balance that teams need if they are to feel confident that they can reach their goals, while still pushing for even greater challenges and missions.

A Crack in the Armor

Maintaining success starts with the details and quickly moves to a broad view. On February 6, 2012, a small crack in the Ivanovo Dam in Bisser, Bulgaria, that had gone unrepaired for years led the dam to burst. Heavy snowmelt had put undue pressure and strain on the fractured area, and, lacking the structural strength to hold back the combined forces of the Arda and Marista Rivers, the dam broke, sending a storm surge almost eight feet high through the villages below. Numerous towns were destroyed by the rise and rush of the currents, and eight people lost their lives.

Most modern dams are built of heavy concrete with steel reinforcement throughout the structure. They are mechanical marvels in terms of the complexity of their construction and their ability to hold back massive external forces from block-aded water flow. When they are operating at peak efficiency, they manage this water flow, protect land regions and structures downriver, and can generate hydroelectric power for the surrounding area.

Great teams functioning in any capacity are like the great dams of the world. They are built with the best materials, reinforced to the very core of their construction, constantly inspected and monitored using the highest standards, and able to manage multiple levels of productive service. But as with the Ivanovo Dam, just one small crack, one tiny breach in the excellence of the team's operations, can cause cataclysmic failure—that is, if the crack goes unchecked.

Teams that allow poor performance, mismanaged leadership, or any other internal or external forces to tear away at their culture of excellence will undoubtedly develop cracks that will grow if they are left unchecked. Your team can either maintain excellence or find itself heading for failure. The larger the fracture, the greater the amount of resources in the form of time, energy, and people it will take to repair the break. The potentially damaging forces that are normally held back by the strength of the team will find the weakness and relentlessly attack. The worst-case scenario is that your team will eventually break under the strain, the resulting deluge will wipe out years of sustained successful efforts, and you will be left to rebuild the team from the ground up.

Successful teams find the point of breach before it occurs. Altering operational requirements and procedures, retraining or replacing personnel, or refocusing resources and efforts in the necessary direction can quickly repair any fracture in your standards of excellence. Remember, the focus of your efforts should always return to mission accomplishment. Don't become overwhelmed by the problem, but remain fixated on the solution. Delays can have serious consequences. When you're dealing with cracks in a dam, any collapse can be catastrophic.

Any team that has experienced success will quickly recognize the signs of faltering and failure. Frequently these signs emanate from a lapse in excellence—excellence in preparedness, excellence in execution, or excellence in evaluation. Clearly, even a small lapse in attention and effort can have devastating consequences. The rest of this chapter will focus on how to maintain success and eliminate the possibility of a small crack maturing into an unstoppable and unmanageable catastrophe.

Maintaining Excellence Through Teamwork

With an understanding that even the smallest cracks can lead to the collapse of your company, it is imperative that you work meticulously to maintain excellence. There is no set equation for preserving your company's prosperity and growth, but you will find that teamwork plays an undeniable role year in and year out.

No matter how it's measured against your efforts, success will ultimately be the by-product of building your team with the top talent, providing these people with a clear purpose, developing their skills to their utmost potential, and executing the necessary tasks that contribute to accomplishing your mission. If you put forth the required focus and energy to develop all these factors under an umbrella of excellence, then you can't help but achieve success. It will inevitably happen.

But any individual who is trying to realize goals on her own is more likely to face the disappointment of adversity and defeat. We are wired to work together. Just like the wolf pack on a hunt, we as people are stronger and more efficient when we collaborate and multiply our own skills and abilities through unified teamwork. In a world in which the limits on resources and external dynamics can at times be downright daunting, excellence is the common bond that can keep your team at the top.

Great teams establish stability and maintain standards through the development of an internal culture that nurtures and encourages success through the principles of teamwork. They never divert their attention from a standard of excellence. You or your industry will define what that standard looks like, but it can never be taken for granted, nor can the team be allowed to slide back into mediocrity. This standard must be internalized by each team member and, at some point, must come to operate from the inside out, rather than being imposed from the top down.

Fisher DeBerry, former head coach of the U.S. Air Force Academy, told me,

> When it comes to maintaining excellence through teamwork, every team and every year is different. Just like in football, those corporations that have been successful have done it year in and year out. I think they're constantly trying to see how they can do things better, in a less expensive manner, and see how they can make more money. You don't rest on your laurels, because the next year everyone starts out the same way: 0–0. So it doesn't make any difference if you won 'em all the year before or lost 'em all the year before; everyone is the same at the beginning of the season.
>
> You've got to find that edge, and that is created by how you've orchestrated things in the off-season or trained your team. You have to challenge every team differently. Each year we had a motto, and we allowed the kids to choose that motto. They'd make recommendations, and we'd discuss the options as a staff. And we would choose a motto we'd saturate the team with. Simultaneously, we would review our previous season and, moving forward, ask ourselves, "What do we have to do to get better?" As long as you have that attitude and impress upon your players that they've never arrived, you will never fall flat on your

laurels. None of us have ever arrived at what we are capable of doing. Let's strive always to be the best we can be and to constantly challenge our teams to want to be good.

The best teams I've been associated with—whether through professional sports, military service, or private endeavors—all had a culture of excellence. They had what Fisher DeBerry instilled into his team. They relied upon one another to establish and maintain the highest quality of execution on their own. To put it simply, the impetus can't come from the coach all the time. At some point your players must take over, maintain the team's standards on their own, and police themselves accordingly. Otherwise, you'll spend an enormous amount of time and energy circling back to reinstitute standards that should be a given. If you manufacture a culture of excellence, that level of independence has the opportunity to occur.

This doesn't mean that excellence shouldn't be underlined and emphasized to your team on a continuing basis. But quality of effort starts with the individual's understanding his role in the context of the team's overall performance and having a desire to never be the weakest link. You'll recognize this in your own team when its members show signs of doing what's right for one another and not what's right for themselves.

This spirit of teamwork as it relates to culture must be passed on from one generation of team members to the next. It emulates past successes and understands the level of effort that was necessary to overcome obstacles in the past. Never lose sight of the focus, unity, and direction "mantra" in building and maintaining excellence in everything you do. Teams that have excellence woven through the core of their identity will develop a culture of success that can withstand any and all competitive hurdles in its path.

When excellence is no longer a goal but an established standard, success will become its exact reflection. To quote from retired NASA space flight director Gene Kranz, "Failure is not an option." And it never will be when your team is led by a culture of internal excellence.

Teams at Work 19: The Transcontinental Railroad—The Golden Spike

The U.S. Congress passed the Pacific Railroad Acts of 1862 and 1864 that made the construction of the transcontinental railroad possible, with the Central Pacific Railroad of California and the Union Pacific Railroad working to merge the two lines from the Atlantic to the Pacific Oceans for the first time. Congress supported the act through U.S. bonds and land grants. The Union Pacific employed laborers from both the Union and Confederate armies (veterans) and Irish immigrants. The Central Pacific employed primarily Chinese immigrants.

> Most of the work consisted of the laying of the rails. The track laying was divided up into various parts: one gang laid rails on the ties, drove the spikes, and bolted the splice bars; at the same time, another gang distributed telegraph poles and wire along the grade, while the cooks prepared dinner and the clerks busied themselves with accounts, records, using telegraph wire to tap for more materials and supplies.

In addition to track laying (which typically employed approximately 25% of the labor force), the operation also required the efforts of hundreds of tunnelers, explosive experts, bridge builders, blacksmiths, carpenters, engineers, masons, surveyors, teamsters, telegraphers, and even cooks, to name just a few of the trades involved in construction of the railroad.

The result was that a distance that had once taken six months to travel now took only six days. It eliminated death, disease, and crime, and it cut weeks to months off travel. It brought people together, increased interstate commerce, and produced a boom in the economy. The last spike placed into the railroad, also known as "the Golden Spike," was inscribed with "May God continue the unity of our Country, as this Railroad unites the two great Oceans of the world." Few can argue that this unification was one of the greatest examples of teamwork in the history of our nation. ("First Transcontinental Railroad," *Wikipedia*, January 22, 2013.)

Creating a Culture of Winning

Maintaining excellence is as vital to the success of your company as achieving it in the first place. In fact, many CEOs and leaders will tell you that being innovative once can be pure luck, but a résumé of innovation is no fluke. The great Green Bay Packers coach Vince Lombardi once said, "Winning is not a sometime thing; it's an all the time thing. You don't win once in a while. You don't do things right once in a while; you do them right all the time. Winning is a habit." Success and winning are why we come together as teams in the first place. We combine our talents and efforts to achieve something that would be unachievable by an individual. Whether it is within your own family, a small business, or a corporate conglomerate, the overall goal is to achieve team success. To go about our lives and our livelihood with any other objective in mind would be to work against our own happiness, if not our very survival.

Achieving success reinforces one's individual purpose, and when that success is achieved by a team, it reinforces the purpose of pooling our efforts. To once again borrow from the famous speech of Lieutenant General George S. Patton, Jr., "When you, here, everyone of you, were kids, you all admired the champion marble player, the fastest runner, the toughest boxer, the big league ball players, and the All-American football players. Americans love a winner. . . . Americans play to win all of the time."

Part of General Patton's message was that winning is synonymous with success. The efforts of a unified army—or "team," as he described it—could not help but be successful. Success breeds confidence, and with confidence comes the ability to achieve extraordinary results. Success strengthens and supports the foundation in the minds of team members for the elements of team building that we've addressed. Nothing reinforces success better than the experience of achieving it.

Successful teams pass on their identity to the individual. The proper context and the realization of the importance of one's role in creating success can provide a sense of pride and personal accomplishment within a team—especially when the leaders acknowledge the efforts, the output, and, at times, the sacrifice of the members who played a part in the achievement.

Chad Hennings is a former defensive lineman for the Air Force Academy and the Dallas Cowboys. After being drafted by the Cowboys, he was part of a team that won three Super Bowls in only four years. When we discussed how teams and corporations succeed year in and year out, he said:

> How do you intend to win year in and year out? As I maintain, it's culture. Being able to have a foundation of who you are, what role you play, what each individual's role is, and to stay focused, and to be able to adapt. Truth is truth. To be able to adapt that foundational aspect doesn't change your character, your integrity, who you are, even, as a team. But the bottom line: there are certain things you have to fine-tune and adjust, and when you go from one leadership style at the top of the pyramid to one that's totally opposite . . . that's when we fall apart.
>
> It's culture, top down: holding your leaders accountable, holding the coaches accountable, coaches holding the veteran leaders accountable, veterans holding the rookies accountable, everyone doing the same thing, and being on the same page. There are huge benefits to excellence, but everybody has to be able to internalize it. These are your core values: this is what we represent; this is what we stand for; this is what we tolerate; this is what we profess; this is who we are as an organization. Those are the lifeblood of our foundational principles. The hope is for a CEO to espouse those and create a corporation where, from the top down, everybody knows those expectations. Then the rest is

*just semantics, execution, and tweaking the tactical things
based upon the environment that you find yourself in.*

Success often presents new opportunities to both the collective team and its members. People want to associate, do business with, and be around or part of successful organizations and teams. Others (teams and individuals) look to successful teams for leadership, both within and outside of their own industries. This explains why so many assistant coaches and personnel from playoff contenders get first crack at new job openings in the National Football League. Owners admire and respect the knowledge and efforts put forth by the members of the most successful teams. They look to those who have experienced success to recreate the culture of winning in their own organizations. Supporting established practices, having pride in identification, and remaining open to new opportunities are all positive effects that this kind of experience can have on team members and their morale.

Avoiding the Pitfalls of Success

Actor Desi Arnaz, who played Ricky Ricardo on the hit television show *I Love Lucy*, said, "Good things do not come easy. The road is lined with pitfalls." Success can give, and success can take away. All too often in the NFL we see young men with the world at their fingertips squander an opportunity for which others would simply kill. Their success provided them with everything they wanted and needed, but in the end, it was too much for them to handle. They made poor decisions with their newfound wealth and found themselves broke and out of the NFL in just a matter of years. The same is true in business. Corporations often find great success quickly, only to make unethical, immoral, or even illegal decisions that can cause them to fail and take millions with them in the process. Think of Enron, WorldCom, and many other modern-day front-runners whose success led them to make less-than-honest decisions that inevitably resulted in failure.

In the short term, success in sports is measured in terms of the season at hand: football teams measure themselves against 16 games, baseball teams against 162, and professional tennis players through tournament elimination. Time is finite. Points are awarded. There are winners and losers. Eventually, the season ends and your team is judged by its positive or negative record. Then the process starts all over again.

Some areas of teamwork don't have such a clear-cut definition of achievement and success. The introduction of a concise mission statement is vital in such ambiguous situations. But some teams just aren't sure what their direction is, even after they receive the stated definition. The journey that got them where they are becomes lost as they attain the destination. Success must be clearly defined to ensure that all the other elements of team building are in their proper place, as a single success can never be the final outcome.

Truly great teams are always looking to improve. When the competition succumbs to their superior efforts, great teams compete against themselves. Every team member understands that "the best" can always be better and that records are made to be broken. Teams that have well-seasoned members and experienced veterans, and also have astute leadership and the proper perspective, are more able to put their success into the context of their ongoing mission. These teams appreciate the contrast of failure and success and the fine line that can sometimes separate the two.

Younger teams without this experience can lose sight of the fact that true success—sustained success—is a marathon and not a sprint. Their members lack the necessary understanding of what it means to maintain focus, create unity, stay true to the path, and operate at the highest level of excellence. Winning, achievement, success—whatever you call your mission accomplishment—can actually act as a force for adversity and failure.

Some team members may not see, understand, or feel a sense of mission fulfillment when they have achieved it. They may ask, "Is this it?" or "What's the point?" They may apathetically remove themselves as cogs and cause the machine to come to a halt.

Sports teams and business ventures aren't the only endeavors that are susceptible to the corrupting forces of success. Over the course of history, entire kingdoms and dynasties have fallen as a result of poor handling of the negative effects of success.

Leaders lose sight of their purpose and become the victims of their own self-importance, seizing the spoils for themselves. Team members lose the context of their roles and feel left out, uninvolved, and unrecognized. The need for attention, the desire for acceptance, the petty jealousies, the internal resentments, and the resulting complacency can all put cracks in the dike.

Some individuals may try to direct the spotlight of success upon themselves for personal advancement and gain. They see the team's prosperity as being a result of their individual efforts and try to capitalize on what they believe is their rightful good fortune. Power, money, and influence are all targeted for the taking.

Perspective becomes distorted: "*My* role is more important." "*I* put forth more effort." "It was *my* idea that got us here." "Where would we be without *me*?" These sentiments are especially difficult when they emanate from the top of your team. Mid- and upper-level leaders can forget their role and responsibilities in the overall framework of operations, instead promoting an elitist attitude and agenda. That, as they say, is when the townspeople storm the castle with pitchforks and torches.

Teams at Work 20: The Channel Tunnel ("Chunnel")

The Channel Tunnel . . . is a . . . 31.4 mile undersea rail tunnel linking Folkestone, Kent, in the United Kingdom with Coquelles, Pas-de-Calais, near Calais in northern France beneath the English Channel at the Strait of Dover. . . .

The tunnel carries high-speed Eurostar passenger trains, Eurotunnel Shuttle roll-on/roll-off vehicle transport—the largest in the world—and international rail freight trains. . . .

The British *Channel Tunnel Group* consisted of two banks and five construction companies, while their French counterparts, *France–Manche*, consisted of three banks and five construction companies. The role of the banks was to advise on financing and secure loan commitments. On 2 July 1985, the groups formed Channel Tunnel Group/France–Manche (CTG/F–M).

Ten construction companies in the CTG/F-M group [did the design and construction]. . . . The five French construction companies in the joint venture group GIE Transmanche Construction [undertook the French terminal and boring]. . . . The five British construction companies in the Translink Joint Venture [undertook the English Terminal and boring]. The two partnerships were linked by TransManche Link (TML), a bi-national project organization. The Maître d'Oeuvre was a supervisory engineering body employed by Eurotunnel under the terms of the concession that monitored project activity and reported back to the governments and banks.

In France, with its long tradition of infrastructure investment, the project garnered widespread approval. . . .

The Channel Tunnel is a build-own-operate-transfer (BOOT) project with a concession. TML would design and build the tunnel, but financing was through a separate legal entity: Eurotunnel. Eurotunnel absorbed CTG/F-M and signed a construction contract with TML; however, the British and French governments controlled final engineering and safety decisions, which are now in the hands of the Channel Tunnel Safety Authority.

Now for the teamwork part of the show. More than 13,000 skilled and unskilled workers were hired to build the Channel Tunnel. Using mining and hole-boring equipment, the work teams started digging from both England and France, intending to meet in the middle as the excavation continued. During the process, 10 construction employees were fatally injured, with the majority of the accidents occurring at the beginning of the project. The actual physical connection in the form of a raw hole was punched through in October 1990. The official ceremony occurred several weeks later amid cameras and media fanfare celebrating the 13,000-person team and its unbelievable accomplishment. ("Channel Tunnel," *Wikipedia*, January 28, 2013.)

Managing Your Successful Team

As a leader, part of your job is to handle success throughout your company to prevent complacency and negative issues. First you reach success, then you manage it. Just like adversity, success should be expected and planned for ahead of time. Communication is paramount for maintaining the context and perspective that we've discussed. Constant, consistent feedback will help team members understand the context of their role in the operational execution that will lead to your achieving your mission statement.

By ensuring that you have a timely, detailed, and ongoing evaluation process, you and your team members will have already developed an appreciation for the areas in which success has been built and in which improvement is warranted. But if ideas are left unspoken, the resulting gaps in communication can become filled with misinterpretation and misrepresentation of efforts. I can't stress this enough. Do the little things early and often in your team's overall process to guarantee that your team doesn't lose its frame of reference or focus on its context for each member.

Successful teams not only evaluate their individual members, but continue to look for new and more efficient ways to improve already proven methods. Challenging team members through self-evaluation can be both a positive and a productive means of enhancing your existing operational procedures.

Those working in specific areas of your team often already know exactly what needs to be done to enhance and improve what is perceived as a successful method, yet their input may never be sought. Change for its own sake isn't necessary, but remember the constant dynamics that are working against you. If your team is already ahead, put it up one step further.

Don't stop the efforts you have already put in place to help you continually train for the future. With your team's newfound or prolonged success come various challenges that may be confronted from different angles, different perspectives, and perhaps with a different purpose. Find ways to help the team members understand and utilize their new position of strength through ongoing exercise training. Put them through new "reaction course" training with the view and vantage point from the top.

Use your success to leverage your position within your industry. Seize this opportunity to position your team members in the critical areas that guide the team's operations: seek to place them on advisory boards or commissions, and encourage them to become involved in panels, study groups, and steering committees.

As general manager of the Denver Broncos, I constantly supported our staff's engaging in similar opportunities within the National Football League. Our scouting department, video operations, and turf management group were all members of

NFL committees that helped formulate policy and provide input on the rules and regulations that guided our efforts.

Remember, most of us don't conclude our team's work at the end of a sports season. We are constantly forced to carry on from the moment we are currently in. At times, that can be through adversity; at other times, in more balanced scenarios, we can carry on from a position of success.

With this in mind, consider the crucial steps that leaders can take to maintain excellence and infuse their teams with the ability to handle success at the highest levels.

Reward Your Team

Reward team members when and where it's deserved, but only based on their performance. Make sure that your top producers are well taken care of. Rainmaker Thinking's Bruce Tulgan emphasizes the need for and importance of "customizing" deals for each member in order to retain the best and the brightest. If your resources and rewards are limited, focus them on the very best members of your team. Go back to the examples you find in nature: the wolf pack allows the "breeding pair" to feed first, and it is normally this pair that works the hardest to bring down the prey.

Pick a Captain

Strongly consider instituting a "captain" program. Most sports teams have captains—usually elected directly by the team members—that act as a conduit for the team members and their concerns. Though various levels of leadership are a must and each should take an active role in the team-building process, nothing might serve you better than to have a few key members whom your team members trust and respect for what they have accomplished. Your captains might be your top producers or your most experienced associates. They, perhaps more than anyone, can help establish, maintain, and develop a culture of success in your team.

Some people may feel that the use of a captain program outside of sports is a bit impractical, but I think it is exactly what is missing in weak teams in all areas. Captains can serve as a direct extension of more formal methods of leadership. They are loyal to the cause and mission of your team, and they can easily convey this by their own examples both within and outside the workplace. When they are selected by their fellow team members and not appointed by the leaders, captains can relate to their peers and communicate issues more honestly.

Find Fresh Talent

Look to shrewdly fortify your team with fresh talent and new ideas, but never stray from the principles of selection discussed earlier. Use as much discretion and care in selecting new team members during successful times as you did when you were initially building your team or retooling it during difficult times. Outside experience and alternative points of view can often provide novel approaches and innovative ideas for maintaining or even expanding your team's success.

It is important for you, as an organization or a team, to acknowledge success and not run from it. You've worked hard to reach the top, and your competition would like nothing better than to knock you off. But if you recalibrate your team's goals and set the bar higher, you'll constantly be chasing yourself to the top of the hill. Your focus will truly be on the journey and not always on the destination.

Communicate

The common thread that runs throughout all efforts at building top teams is communication. It seems that a great deal is said in times of crisis, but little in times of prosperity. Treat both failure and success in the same balanced manner. Always look for ways to improve by constructing a consistent means of communicating new ideas within your team's culture, looking for excellence in every facet of your team's operations, and giving your team members the means, the methods, and the responsibility to act on their own.

In my interview, Jeff Pash, NFL vice president and executive counsel, told me the following:

> *What I've found that really motivates team members year in and year out to truly be great is the opportunity to continue to grow. We do not live in the 1950s or the 1960s, where you assume that you will be with a company for your entire working life. I don't think most of these people have come to the NFL with the expectation that it'll be the only place they work.*
>
> *For us to assume that we hire someone when he's 30 and he's going to be with us for the next 30 years is unrealistic. But what we do want to do is keep people fresh,*

challenged, and excited and make it clear to them that they are going to have continued opportunities to grow, not just as lawyers, but as businesspeople and managers. They'll handle budgets, supervise outside counsel, and supervise younger attorneys. And so their responsibilities will broaden from handling basic trademark registrations, to doing the negotiations on intellectual property in increasingly complex settings, to handling not just the negotiations but the entire business terms of the negotiations.

And they'll get to the point where they'll be the attorneys giving the presentation to the owners. That kind of thing keeps people excited and interested, and able to see their own growth and progress, and it obviously comes with greater compensation and recognition. To me, that's what young people are looking for: opportunity. These young people are extraordinarily talented, and they've been exposed to so much more than most of us had been at that age. I think one thing they are entitled to that they often don't get enough of is respect. To keep your team members motivated and successful year in and year out, you have to respect them and give them the opportunity to be truly excellent.

An Apple a Day Maintains Excellence

On April Fool's Day, 1976, Steve Jobs, Steve Wozniak, and Ronald Wayne established Apple Computer. Over the following four decades, Apple Inc. has been a primary force in the development and distribution of personal computers and consumer electronics worldwide. To build a company as diverse and influential as Apple has certainly taken an immense amount of teamwork in the development, production, distribution, and marketing of its products.

Most of us associate Apple with dominance in the electronics industries, and certainly the company is at the forefront of how we answer the phone, listen to music, read books, and organize our lives. But this technological giant has gone through its own peaks and valleys on its way to the top as a corporate team. Innovation in management style, creativity in product development, and a firm sense of its own history, in conjunction with a vision of its future, seem to have kept Apple continually moving ahead.

Those teams that operate in the world of technology know that today's "new" is tomorrow's "old" and therefore are constantly looking forward, even as they achieve present success. Apple created a team made up of the very best and brightest at what they do, implemented innovative programs to award its highest achievers, and hasn't been afraid to tinker with and tailor its leadership to the times and needs of the team. As a result, it continues to produce the very best in high-tech consumer products and remains one of the most valuable companies in the world.

Like that of Apple, the culture you build to envelop your team will sustain your success and maintain an environment of accomplishment, even after you have reached important milestones. An established culture creates a codified identity for your team: "This is who we are. This is how we do things. This is why we operate."

A team that never loses sight of its identity will never lose sight of its mission and will always strive to be better and go farther. Teams that put careful thought and consideration into how they go about recruiting talent, establishing goals, developing skills, finding the right fits, providing direction, handling adversity, and dealing with success have already put the framework of their culture into place. It's who you are, how you do things, and why you do them.

Steve Jobs returned to Apple in 1997 to help turn its fortunes around. He understood the principles that the company was founded on because he had helped create them. Your team will have its own members (past and present) who appreciate and identify with the philosophies that led to the team's success. Reach out and embrace this experience. Don't be afraid of your successful past. Use it to guide your team toward continued accomplishments.

CONCLUSION

I once spoke at a business seminar aimed at training young entrepreneurs in the latest techniques of management and team building. A young woman who was starting her first enterprise approached me after my presentation and asked me, "What's the single most important thing you have learned during all your years of working with teams?"

I paused for a moment and really thought about what she'd asked. My mind flashed back to the years I had spent as a collegiate football player at the Air Force Academy, as head coach of the academy's prep school, as a bobsledder for the U.S. National Team leading up to the 1988 Winter Olympics, as flight commander of a group of highly skilled professionals in Air Force Intelligence during the Cold War, as director of college scouting with the Denver Broncos over back-to-back Super Bowl championships, and then finally as general manager of the club I had devoted 16 years to helping build into one of the best teams in the National Football League.

"Caring," I said. "What's most important is caring about the mission of the team and the people who are trying to help fulfill that mission—players, coaches, scouts, staff, airmen— more than about myself." Only when you grasp the concept of compassion and caring for the bigger picture can you truly understand what teamwork is about.

When you put the goals and aspirations of your team and its players ahead of everything else, you can achieve just about anything—and your own individual achievements will ultimately be attained tenfold.

This includes:

o   Caring to spot the best and the brightest in your industry and assembling the top "playmakers" who can give your team a moral fabric and a skill set woven of steel rather than straw.

o   Caring to communicate a clear and concise "mission statement" that flows easily from your FUDES for thought throughout the entire organization.

o   Caring to develop your team members to their fullest capacity in order to allow them to perform at peak levels and grow within the structure and framework of the team.

o   Caring to show the necessary patience and flexibility in order to find the right fit and placement for each and every productive member.

o   Caring to provide the essential direction, context, and guidance to execute your team's plan in both short- and long-term operations.

o   Caring to help your team survive adversity and learn the lessons from defeat that ultimately strengthen a team and make it more resilient over the long haul.

o   Caring to challenge your team members to maintain levels of excellence so that they don't become complacent and succumb to the inevitable pitfalls that can divide even the greatest of champions.

Putting the needs of the group ahead of your own is a very tall order in today's "get as much as I can" society. Teamwork and loyalty seem to be almost quaint.

But my mind flashes again to a service academy football program that went from 2–9–1 to 10–2 in just four short years. I think of my "rookie season" as head coach of the Air Force Prep Huskies, the Colorado Football Conference champions. I see myself flying down the track in Winterburg, West Germany, in hopes of becoming one of the three sleds on the U.S. Winter Olympic Team. I recall the tense moments of tracking Soviet fighters that were scrambling to intercept one of our surveillance missions over the Baltic Sea. I vividly see John Mobley, a Division II linebacker out of tiny Kutztown State and a player I had pushed hard to select in the first round of the 1996 NFL Draft, knock down the final pass to win Super Bowl XXXII for the Denver Broncos.

The fundamental principles of building strong teams that have been discussed in this book work. They have helped Ed Roski build a billion-dollar business, Majestic Realty. They have guided Dr. Charlie Palmer in training wildland firefighters. They have served as the foundation for Vern Abila's security operations around the globe. They were the bedrock for Dr. Harvey Schiller's long and storied career in executive management. And they made Coach Fisher DeBerry and Coach Tom Osborne two of the most respected men in college football.

I'm certain that if you take your own passion and apply it to these same principles of team building, using the various techniques and processes we have outlined, you too will take your team to the top.

INDEX

ABOUT THE AUTHOR

Ted Sundquist is the former General Manager of the Denver Broncos and helped build that NFL organization for 16 years (1992–2008). He played football at the United States Air Force Academy (1980–1983).

A former Air Force officer and member of the U.S. Bobsled team, Sundquist is a football analyst working with NFL Network and Altitude Sports. He appears on such national sports programs as ESPN's "Outside the Lines" and Sirius XM radio, and he writes about football management and leadership for his blog www.TheFootballEducator.com. Sundquist sits on the Board of Directors for the U.S. Air Force Academy Athletic Foundation.

He and his wife Amy reside in Parker, Colorado.